TEARS
OF THE LONELY

TEARS
OF THE LONELY

Ayo Oyeku

afternoon. But the eyes and lips had remained. The boy began to peer closer at the organs. His mind raced beyond the hills and rivers. His heart thudded heavily against his chest. Suddenly, a great strength rejuvenated his whole being. He held unto it. Quickly, he turned away from the cashew tree and fled to the market.

His hasty arrival into the market was unnoticed. The hustling and bustling of the market ignored his consciousness. He heaved a sigh of great relief and calmed down, as he pushed his way through the busy market.

The immense Kajola market was most busy on Saturdays. It was the market day. On this day, things were sold at an exclusively cheap rate. And the villagers took advantage of this day to buy things in stock. Belonging to the people of Kajola, yet, the market was shared with people from the neighbouring village; Irewolu. The two villages fostered a healthy relationship by trading with one another at the market. The boy was from Irewolu.

The sun descended upon the market atmosphere. It radiated heat from its core and stung the people with its arrows. The breeze blew hotly against the perspiring bodies. Traders and buyers sweated under the sun. Buyers haggled angrily with the persuasive traders, and threatened to leave, hurrying to flee from the wrath of the vengeful element, smiling at them in the clouds. Still, gossip was at its peak, as some people cared less about the scorching sun.

"Good afternoon, mama."

The little boy stopped in front of a large, old counter. Wet vegetables were arranged on the counter. Water dripped from the vegetables unto the dusty market floor. A large quantity of melon seeds were evenly scattered across the old counter. The old woman's eyes blinked in cognizance of the boy.

"Good afternoon, my son. How is your mother?"

"She is well. Home is well too." The boy responds generally.

He wasn't a stranger to the generous, old woman. He knew she would take her dutiful time to ask after everyone in his family. Enunciating her words carefully and simultaneously delaying the young boy. Since he had answered her next, likely question, he quickly declares his purpose, before the old woman thought of what to say.

"Mother needs some melon seeds," the boy cuts in.

Ignoring his demand, the old woman stoops low. She sticks her neck out of the counter, peering closely at the boy.

"Are you not the child born to Amope seven festivals back?" She enquired.

"Yes, Mama," he replied quickly.

"Oh! You have grown so big."

She remarked gleefully; clasping her wrinkled palms against her chest. She stared at the boy in total surprise. The young boy fidgeted with his fingers to hold back his impatience. The old woman had seen him three days back, and asked the same question. And she had also reacted the same way. The boy watched her throat, as she mumbled to herself. The weak flesh around her throat contracted and threatened to snap at the slightest strain.

"Mother needs some melon seeds."

He repeated, more calmly. He stretched the money in his hand towards her. He heaved a sigh of relief as the old woman collected the money. The senility of her senescence took toll on her trading process. The boy patiently watched, as she slowly packed the required quantity of melon seeds in a large leaf.

"You can have this too, my son."

The boy had flung his hands frontward to collect his pack of melon seeds. But the generous woman filled his vacant palms with some groundnuts. He could not reject her kind gesture. He smiled at her. He thanked her, meekly. And he stuffed the groundnuts into his left pocket.

"This is for your mother."

She handed over the melon seeds to the boy. He collected it from her and turned to leave. The old woman began sending continuous greetings to Amope. The boy assured to convey her greetings as he walked slowly away from her stall. She was now asking for a remembrance of the boy's name, when he vanished from sight.

The young boy walked as fast as his tiny legs could carry him. The old woman had delayed him, and he was sure his dear mother would have been waiting for him by now. He hurried along the bush path. It seemed as if all the air in the bush followed him. It blew into every part of him. He dashed his right feet against recalcitrant stones that hindered his pace. Pelting them away, as red dusts settled on his feet.

"Okiki"

The call darted towards him like a fired arrow; piercing through his bones and marrows. It sent a chill down his spine. He could feel his feeble legs fractioned against one another. His name had been called. The call was soft, but piercing. He had heard the similar voice. He turned his head. He was standing towards the cashew tree again. He was certain that it was a call from the mysterious tree.

The vengeful sun slid behind the rocky clouds. The atmosphere changed with rapid fervour. And the breeze came, dropping in small packets. It made him shudder a little. Another sizeable packet of breeze hit him towards the chest. It tore through his tender heart and caressed his soul. He became calm. He was fully aware of what was happening around him.

The elephant grasses by the bush path seemed to close up on him. It embraced him into a confident posture. He clenched his fists. Holding unto every atom of air he could grasp. His palm began to ache. But he clawed at the fragile melon seeds. Then the wind came rushing towards him. It blew vehemently at him. Crippled stones rattled across the ground. Red dusts grew wings and mounted on the invisible strata of the air.

The heavy wind flung the branches of the cashew tree wide. Its leaves swayed loosely. And some of the ripe cashew fruits dropped to the ground. The leaves twirled around Okiki. He did not shrug them off. He allowed them to caress his body. Lost in the rhapsody, Okiki opened up to the embrace of the tree. The rushing winds escaped behind the bushes. All became still.

"You can have them."

The cashew tree's branches swung low, as he heard. He looked at the direction. Right at the root of the tree were some cashew fruits. They were scattered all over. He could not resist the temptation. He thought of the pleasurable satiation he would derive from the fruits. But his sanctimonious sanctity would not let him. He shrugged off the impetuosity that weighed on his shoulders. He turned to leave.

"Okiki please, I want you to have them."

The persuasive words of the cashew tree sailed slowly into his ears. A feeling of guilt beclouded him. Unless he took some of the fruits, he was certain that the kind tree would not be pleased with him. Taking careful steps, he moved towards the tree. He bent down and picked some of the cashew fruits. The shadow of the tree enveloped him; soothing away his fears. Okiki stood up, facing the tree. He opened his mouth to express his gratitude. But the words refused to come out. The tentacles of innocence in his bowels pulled at the words clutching to his throat. The encounter mystified him.

"Go home. Mother calls you."

The cashew tree told him. Immediately, Okiki became conscious of time. He realized how expectant his mother would be by then. Hurriedly, he pushed some of the fruits into his pockets. He packed the melon seeds firmly in his hands and dashed away. He ran as swiftly as he could, gathering much winds and dusts back to the village.

Amope, a fair-skinned robust woman was standing on her toes, awaiting the arrival of her last child. A soft crumple below her eyes told she was in her late forties. The once beautiful woman stood in front of her hut. The blurring silhouette of a person afar off materialized into Amope's dearest child. A soft anger welled up within her, as her fears were allayed.

"You are late!" Amope remarked sharply.

Okiki stood before his mother, puffing away the warm air from his bowels. His face wore guilt and fear. He did not know how to explain what had transpired in the past few minutes. He hated offending his beloved mother. He remained silent. Amope snatched the melon seeds from him. And she walked briskly away from him. She did not want to vent her anger on him. He followed timidly. His steps were barely heard.

Amope drew a large wooden tray from a corner of her room. She spread the melon seeds on it. She carried this to the backyard. And found a suitable spot to place the tray for sunning. Okiki watched from a safe distance. He thought of how to assuage his mother's feelings towards him.

"Mother, the old woman gave me some groundnuts." The guilty child spoke, timidly.

"That's kind of her," Amope replied.

Okiki dipped his hands into his pockets to reveal the groundnuts. Amope pretended to be scattering the melon seeds on the tray. But she watched him with the corner of her eyes. As he forced some of the groundnuts out of by the nausea as he watched his wife walk towards the backyard. A further glance at Amope would instigate him to wrought evil. Adigun knew this.

"I am off to see Kasali." Adigun hollered.

The bamboo chair creaked as he stood up. He flung his native shirt, which had been hanging on the arm of the chair, unto his left shoulder. His departure unleashed some cooling breeze into the hut. The children looked at one another and smiled. Amope didn't notice their expression, otherwise she would have queried.

The children finished their meal and joined their mother at the backyard. Debisi packed the bowls together and began washing. Doja, the eldest son, a neatly built young man with a rough moustache, sat beside his mother under the cooking shed. He was in his late twenties. Okiki squatted by the doorstep, gazing at the yolk of the moon. He was certain his father wouldn't return until when darkness choked up the moon.

"Mother, I do not like the way father looks at you."

Doja commented quietly into the night. He did not look at his mother. Instead, he ran his forefinger through the soft sand, which glittered under the moonlight. Okiki was attentive. Amope understood Doja's question. She knew what he was driving at. She brooded over a suitable response.

"Time would heal the wounds." She replied tersely.

Okiki had to stick out his ears to listen to the soft words uttered from the cavity of lowliness. Doja was infuriated by his mother's reply. He was the spearhead of the family, and was ready to stand for his mother's interests. He wondered over when the accurate timing would be. The unleashed serpent had been spitting its cantankerous venom for so long. And Doja wanted to curb this.

"How long, mother?" Doja demanded harshly.

His voice echoed into the night. Still, he didn't turn to look at his mother. But his finger had ceased to move. Okiki could not comprehend the argument. Debisi had finished washing; she also sat quietly on a heap of sand, watching the two. Amope resented her husband's feelings towards her. But she wouldn't allow her children to grow ill feelings towards their benefactor. She remained quiet. The atmosphere was becoming tense. Doja wasn't getting any response from his mother. Debisi began to breathe intermittently, afraid of what might proceed from her elder brother's mouth. A hot breeze seemed to hover above their heads. Okiki was also becoming uncomfortable. Doja was about blurting out when the lowly voice changed the forlorn night.

"Be patient. My son; be patient."

Amope's remark touched the soft spot of Doja. She pulled him close to her bosom and caressed his head. Doja succumbed, hating himself. Like a magical wand, soft breezes began blowing again behind Adigun's hut. Okiki sighed, as peace reigned. Doja knew his mother had kicked the serpent under the mat. He must kill it before an inevitable harm was done. But he would wait for the right time. Time must judge.

"Mother, guess what happened at the farm today?"

Debisi, Amope's only daughter cut in. A chip off the old 'block, Debisi resembled her mother in every way. She was a fair-skinned, robust lady; with a silhouette skin. Anyone could easily misjudge Debisi's voice for her mothers'. They were two of a kind. People admired them for their exceptional beauty.

"Tell me, my daughter."

Amope replied and a beautiful conversation began. Doja was not exempted, as he joined in the discussion. They spent the night exchanging stories and banters. Passers-by and neighbours could hear the hilarious laughter coming from the back of Adigun's hut. Okiki had also participated in the funfair, until he was overridden by his thoughts. The little boy began to ponder over the day's experience. He thought about the old cashew tree. He could still remember the whole scene, vividly. Okiki's mind raced into the legendary stories he had heard about the existence of the Supreme Being.

"Come!"

His reflections were cut short by the voice. Okiki had heard the call again. He wouldn't mistake the tree's voice for anything else. The audible voice was soft, bold and calling. He recognized the voice at once. He looked through the dark hut, and saw the cashew tree standing at a considerable distance in front of the hut. He was surprised. The cashew tree hadn't shared the statue-still nature of trees. It was peripatetic. Okiki wondered what it had come to do.

The call was repeated. Okiki obliged and got up. He took a step at a time, as he advanced towards the tree. The closer he drew, the brighter the cashew tree became. He saw that a cluster of stars encircled the tree. Its sight was glorious and majestic. Suddenly, a vista of events opened before him. He began to view all he had done during the day. A hammer of guilt plunged into his heart when he saw his misdeed: He had thrown the cashew fruits away. His heart began beating heavily. Okiki now understood why the generous cashew tree had come. He began to jitter on how to justify his reason for throwing away the fruits.

He realized a force was now pulling him towards the tree that conjures. He tried to pull back but couldn't. The cluster of stars reappeared as mean, bewitching eyes. The billowing branches materialized as beastly fangs. Okiki was sickened by terror.

"Okiki, get up and go inside."

He heard another voice. It was sharp and familiar. He flicked his eyes open. And saw his mother addressing him. He looked through the hut and saw darkness. He had been lost in a mist of illusion and fear. Amope had seen him dozing.

"Go inside and sleep."

Amope repeated firmly. The young boy stood up and went inside.

2

Large Heart

S HE BROUGHT THE melon seeds down from the lower roof. It was three days back Amope sent her last child to buy it. As soon as the sun rose fully in the afternoon, Amope spread the melon seeds on a large, wooden tray. She sprinkled some water on the seeds, till they all got wet. She did this to enable easy removal of the melon seeds from its skin. Amope found a stool at a shaded corner of the backyard. She called for Okiki as she sat down. Okiki emerged and he understood his mother wanted him to assist her with the peeling.

"Be careful this time." She warned him firmly.

Okiki remembered that the last time he peeled melon seeds; he had broken most of the seeds in two. He wondered what difference it made if the seeds were broken or not, after all, it would still be grounded on the grinding stone. Okiki understood his mother was superfluous with the arts and crafts of cooking, and everything had to be in the right order. The little boy sat next to his mother, peeling the seeds with caution and care.

Melon soup was Adigun's favourite. He enjoyed it most with pounded yam. During the primal years of their wedlock, he showered praises on his wife after consuming the meal with obvious relish. Amope's expertise in preparing the meal did not wane with the years. But the admiration and love they often shared faded with time. Adigun still relished his favourite meal. But he would not be cajoled into loving his wife anymore. The dearth of love was born by a strange sickness. This sickness began to torture Amope's soul, seven months after the birth of Okiki. Adigun would not tolerate this. Every day he crafted every means to stay away from the woman he had once swore to protect throughout his entire life. Time had changed yesterday.

"You know this is your father's favourite?" Amope teased. Okiki smiled back. Little did his mother know that this was his favourite too?

"Finish up with the remaining seeds while I set the yams on fire."

Amope got up and hurried towards the cooking shed. Okiki began to salivate as he thought about the meal.

Hurriedly, he peeled the few remaining seeds on the tray. In the process, he broke some of the seeds. Afraid of instigating his mother's anger, he quickly hid the broken seeds in his pockets.

Amope was enraptured by the halcyon days she once shared with her husband. Her face wore a smile. Good memories were livened anytime she prepared this particular meal. It gave her hope. She believed things would still change for good.

"Time is not on our side."

Amope encouraged. Okiki finished up and hurried to the cooking shed. He stoked the flames and Amope watched. As soon as the yams got boiled, Okiki threw them into the mortar and Amope pounded them with all gracefulness and skill. Okiki watched.

Adigun's arrival was timely. Barely fifteen minutes after the meal was prepared. Amope was pleased. Her calculations were right. Adigun enjoyed the dish most when the doughy meal of pounded yam was still very hot. Okiki was most satisfied about his father's early arrival. The worms in his belly had been gesticulating noisily. He was famished.

Adigun sat in his usual position. He waited for his meal to be served. Amope appeared with two sizeable bowls of meal. Adigun was surprised when he saw his favourite meal. He removed his top cloth and hanged it across the bamboo chair, as he always did. The children also hurried to get their meals. Okiki also found a suitable corner in the hut and began eating. The meal turned out to be as delicious as expected. Doja and Debisi also swallowed their meals with obvious relish. They all concentrated on their meals, while Amope was at the backyard, tidying up.

A sour look crawled upon Adigun's face. He caught sight of the unusual. A strand of hair curled across the surface of the soup. Evil intentions raced across his mind. He believed his wife must have been planning to take his life. A fury wind engulfed him.

"Amope" Adigun shouted.

All the children were startled by the shout. They paused to know what went wrong. Amope was also shocked. She could sense trouble was around the corner. She braced up. And she hurried into the hut.

"Here I am, my lord."

"What is this?" Adigun barked.

He pointed towards the hair strand in the soup. Amope was bewildered. She began apologizing convulsively. The children were yet to grasp the whole scene. They kept staring at their parents. Amope gestured to take the soup away but before she could do this, Adigun carried the bowl of soup and splashed it across his wife's face.

The children were shocked. Amope screamed in pains. Her face was stained with the peppery soup. Adigun, had now sprung to his feet, and was accusing his wife of attempting to poison him. Amope staggered blindly before her husband. The helpless woman's hand caught her husband's top, hanged across the bamboo chair. Infuriated, Adigun threw a violent slap across her face. The woman who had earlier been in a Stygian darkness staggered backwards, and hit her back against the rough wall, before falling down.

"Stop father!" Doja shouted from the corner where he sat.

The young man was furious. Doja hated seeing his father laying his hands on his mother. Debisi, who couldn't bear watching her mother being beaten either, jumped to her feet, and hurried to save Amope. Doja equally sprang up and hurried to protect his mother. The hut was in a frightful mess. Adigun still boiled with anger. Certain that his eldest son was against him, he washed his hands, flung his cloth around his neck, and stormed out of the hut.

A miasma of immature repression swept over Okiki. He was stunned. A fistful of pounded yam clung to his throat. His mouth was thrown agape. The physical attack on Amope's womanhood sent an electrifying chill down Okiki's spine. He kept staring, as a clove of tear rolled down his right eye.

Amope wailed. Doja and Debisi led her to the backyard. She staggered blindly along. Tears flowed freely down Amope's face, as Debisi washed her face. Doja was furious. He kept scratching his head, unable to think properly. Amope later calmed down. She looked at her blouse; the melon soup had also soiled it. She signified that she needed to change her clothes, and they allowed her to go into her room. Doja and Debisi returned into the hut.

Amope reappeared soon in fresh clothes, sitting at a lonely corner. The atmosphere in the hut was lachrymose.

Everyone kept silent. Debisi busied cleaning up the mess on the floor. Doja belched with anger and displeasure. He wanted to query his mother. He threw strong glances at her. But Amope averted her eyes. She avoided the unanswerable questions that had welled up in her first child. Debisi sat down when she was through. There was silence. But there wasn't peace.

"Where is Okiki?"

Amope's coarse voice sent a surge across the room. They all stared blankly at one another. Truly, Okiki was missing. He had escaped out of the hut when Amope was being led to the backyard. Half conscious, he ran as fast as he could. The sharp breeze tore through his being. He wished he never saw all that happened.

"Coward"

He could hear his heart telling him. Strong feelings etched at his forehead. He began to ponder if truly he had acted like a coward. His father had just abused his mother. He wondered about what he was supposed to have done. He cried as he ran. His pace reduced as approached the cashew tree. He fell at the root of the tree, and sobbed.

The atmosphere around the cashew tree was portentous. The wind flaunted its wings in varied directions. Soft sands were swept under the sod. Okiki could smell the dust. He stopped crying and lay still. The leaves swayed harmoniously. Okiki was enthralled by the ethereal situation. His pains seemed to be assuaged. A cashew fruit broke free, and hit his scruff. He looked up.

"When the trees cry, who listens to their sobs?"

Okiki was sure to have heard the tree's voice. The words sailed slowly upon the rivers of his emotions. He had to ponder over the question. "Do the trees cry?" Okiki thought to himself. He was unable to decipher the riddle. Another vacuum of silence engulfed the atmosphere. The clouds were scurrying away from the sky. And the night was lurking behind the firmament.

"Large heart . . . Okiki, you need a large heart." The mysterious tree replied. Confused, Okiki stared into emptiness. His earlier question had not been answered. The cashew tree was now imparting a strange knowledge he could not fathom.

"I need a large heart?"

Okiki mumbled the words to himself. He felt lost in the labyrinth of life. He still pondered on the two words. "Was that the solution to his problems?" He thought. Even if it was, he still needed profound understanding to apply this truth.

"Go home. Mother calls you." The cashew tree said.

Okiki came back to total consciousness. The cashew tree was witty and quick at speech. Okiki wanted to query further, but realized that his mother and siblings must have been worried about his sudden disappearance from the hut. He had to return home quickly. He got up, rubbed the dusts around his knees and elbows, and walked back home hastily.

A familiar figure appeared in front of Kasali's hut. Kasali was having his supper when the figure stepped into his hut. Surprised, Kasali wasn't expecting to see his friend at that time. Most importantly, his friend's countenance was tremulous. He stopped eating and asked.

"Hope all is well?"

"All is not well."

Adigun's replied sharply, his voice was harsh. His face seemed to crumple at every parchment on his face. He found a vacant stool in the hut and sat heavily on it. Kasali observed that the precision of his friend's heartbeat was abnormal. He swallowed the last morsel of food and flushed it down with some water.

"Asake, take this food away." Kasali spoke loudly.

Asake; Kasali's wife, appeared from the back of the hut. She was also surprised to see Adigun. Asake greeted him and asked after his wife and children. Adigun's warm response accompanied Asake, as she carried the empty bowls off to the backyard.

"Let's go out."

Kasali got up as he spoke, picking his teeth with a broomstick. Adigun responded, and they walked out of the hut. Adigun and Kasali's friendship had spanned over decades. Like the stars cluster across the sky every night, the two were inseparable. They shared common opinions. And difficult issues were resolved over calabashes of palm-wine.

The palm-wine grove wore its usual manner: Noisy and untidy. Most of the village men spent their evenings at this joint. This was where they took relaxation over the heavy day's work. As jokes and banters swayed from one end to another, Freudian slips were high at its peak. A few women were also present there: shameless concubines of ignoble characters.

Kasali and Adigun took seat on a bench whose legs looked rather groggy. Iya Sadi; the palm-wine-seller emerged with a keg of palm-wine and two empty calabashes. She placed the drink before them and left. The two friends were enraptured by the way Iya Sadi's big buttocks recoiled and vibrated under marching steps. Her robust buttocks never bored them, despite their regular visits. Probably that was her charm for enticing every man in the village to her palm-wine grove.

Kasali filled the calabashes with palm-wine. The palm-wine was very white, with a thick froth on top. They watched the bubbles with a thirsty fervour. Hurriedly, the two friends sipped some of it. Their whole dentition was stiffened by the highly fermented palm-wine. They both grinned affirmatively; Iya Sadi never disappointed them, her palm-wine was not diluted. They enjoyed it most. And they easily got drunk by it.

"I am tired of that woman."

Adigun tapers the mood of the evening, as the evening descends slowly behind the village. Kasali remained quiet. He stared blankly into the frothing palm-wine. Adigun stares at his friend and bellows,

"She attempted to poison me this afternoon!"

"Impossible!" Kasali snaps back.

"Her children also supported her," Adigun added.

"You must handle them with iron fists." Kasali replied.

"Even Doja now threatens to beat me."

"Sacrilege" Kasali shouted.

He became inconvenient on the bench. He shrugs and adjusts. Concerned about his friend's domestic affairs, he persuades Adigun to handle the matter with care and caution. Majority of the drinkers seemed to be affected by the same ailment. Engrossed in their discussions, they all complained bitterly about their wives.

Adigun and Kasali were distracted by a discussion between Iya Sadi and one of her male customers. She was serving him some palm-wine when the man challenged her.

"I am tired of my wife."

"You men are always tired of your wives." Iya Sadi replied.

"No, my own case is pathetic."

"A keg of palm-wine will calm you down."

"No, palm-wine won't solve this."

"What then is the solution?"

"I need another wife."

"What do you need another wife for?"

Iya Sadi was displeased by the man's opinion. She stared at him, leaning her hands over her large breasts. She knew the man was already getting drunk, but she pressed further. Instead, the man responds,

"Would you accept my proposal?"

"What proposal?"

Her mind travels into the man's request. Understanding what he meant, she hissed and retorts "You must be drunk."

The man bursts into laughter. He tries to grab the edge of her wrapper. But she quickly stole away from sight. Adigun and Kasali's eyes meet. Similar thoughts raced through both minds. But Kasali picks the calabash and slurps some palm–wine. Adigun paused for a while, before he finally said,

"I need a second wife."

Adigun took a glance at his friend after making the proposition. He knew how important it was for his friend to agree with his request. Kasali likewise threw a decisive glance at his friend, knowing he had raised a specious decision. He already knew what was on his friend's mind. He smiled coyly and replied.

"Are you sure about this?"

"Yes." Adigun affirmed quickly.

He was now certain that his friend supported him. He swats some gluttonous flies away from the brim of his calabash. He gulps some palm-wine down in satiation. Then there was an impure silence. Kasali's gesture was pregnant with words. Adigun could easily tell his friend still had something to say about that matter or something related; by the way he shrugged and rolled his eyes.

"What else is the matter?" Adigun snaps at his friend.

""What about my own request?" Kasali demanded.

Adigun stares at his friend. He tried to remember what the perpetual request was. The floating moon flashed memories across his face. It had been over a year that Kasali had been persuading him about his nubile daughter. Kasali wanted Debisi to be his second wife. Adigun would not agree to this. Not even a drum of palm-wine would change his mind. His reason was best known to him.

"Forget about that!" He replied sharply.

Kasali smiled with the corner of his mouth. He was certain to fulfil his desire, either by plea or trick. The two men drank in silence.

The moon was fully-grown across the sky. It mounted its wings on the invisible clouds of the night. It illuminated the silent village. Dutiful servants of libation: Adigun and Kasali rose up to go, fully drunk. They sauntered to the rhythms of intoxication. They staggered all the way home, chanting traditional songs with a vague tempo. Their voices echoed through the night. When they reached the cross road, they parted ways and bade each other a good night.

Okiki was almost home when he met his elder brother; Doja, on the way. Doja was glad to find his little brother. Doja had a strong likeness for his little brother, not because he was the second son in the family, neither was it because Okiki was the last child. Doja knew there was something unexplainably special about his cute, soft spoken, innocent brother.

"Okiki, mother is already getting worried about you."

"I am sorry, brother." Okiki replied sheepishly.

Doja did not bother to press Okiki about his disappearance. There was no need revisiting the ugly issue. He could see the weariness on his face. Doja lifted Okiki on his shoulders. And they hurried back home.

"Okiki, where have you been?" Amope queried softly, as they came in. Okiki ran towards his beloved mother and prostrated before her.

"Am sorry my mother."

Amope decided not to ask anymore. She was already exhausted. Okiki pitied her. He slowly dragged his feet into the room to lie down. But he could not sleep. He rolled on the mat, thinking about the wickedness inflicted on his mother. Okiki could tell she had put in a lot of effort in preparing the dish, only for it to be wasted in such an ugly manner. After a short while, seeing it was getting too late and their father was not yet in sight, Doja and Debisi joined Okiki in the room, and they slept off. Okiki lay still on his mat, pretending to be asleep. He awaited his father's arrival.

The darkness at night soon encroached on every visible part of the hut. But Amope waited endlessly for her husband to return. She did not doze or blink an eye. Only a thin ray of moonlight ran through the hut. It was visible enough for one to grope in the darkness. Amope had decided not to put on the lamp in order not to wake up the sleeping children.

Adigun's late emergence blocked the ray of light. He staggered in, heavily drunk. Okiki strained hard to see.

Amope ran towards him and knelt before him, holding his leg.

"Please, my husband." She begged.

"Don't touch me!" Adigun snapped back, drunkenly.

He wrestled his leg free. Amope fell backwards. Okiki felt a surge sweep through him. He clawed at his sleeping-wrapper. Amope wanted to persuade further. But Adigun lifted his hands in indignation. He did not want to hear her voice. Neither did he want his wife to touch him. He stormed into his room. Amope sat hopelessly on the floor. And she cried silently.

Okiki remembered his discussion with the omniscient cashew tree. The old tree had asked him about who ever heard the sobs of the trees. This was still difficult for him to ponder over. Even if he could not hear the sobs of the trees, he could hear his mother in the main hut, sniffling, to hold back the tears. He stared at the roof. A hot tear rolled down the side of his face.

— 3 —

Finding Love, Finding Dream

S HE HAD ASKED Debisi to buy some okra at the market. Doja's ears pricked up, as soon as he heard. Okra soup was his favourite. He could already imagine himself enjoying the mucilaginous vegetable soup. But Debisi wasn't an expert at choosing the fresh type of okras that would make the soup taste as gooey as he wanted, and he knew this.

"Mother, I volunteer." Doja cuts in.

Amope's face lit with surprise. She burst into a smile. She took her firstborn's gesture as an unwarranted act of generosity. And so she declined.

"I insist." Doja re-affirmed.

Amope couldn't help but wonder. Even Debisi was startled by her elder brother's kind gesture. Doja persisted, and yet he refused to tell them the reason behind his decision. Amope and Debisi's eyes gleamed with mockery. A feeling transpired between both women that the market place was Doja's rendezvous with his secret lover.

"I hope your friends would not insult us for sending you; a grown man, to the market?"Amope teased.

"Mother," Doja felt embarrassed.

"Or do you have a hidden agenda?" Debisi quickly adds.

"Shut up!" Doja snaps back, with a big frown on his face.

He would not tolerate any form of mockery from his younger sister. Amope silenced Debisi, and apologized to Doja. She hands over the money to Doja, who hurriedly leaves for the market. When Doja was far from sight, Amope scolded Debisi for attempting to let the cat out of the bag. Doja's reaction already proved that their guesses were right. They began to laugh over the matter.

Doja whistled all the way to the market. He passed by the old cashew tree. The cashew tree called his name, but he did not hear. Everything around the market bore resemblance with a masquerade carnival. Buyers hastily moved from stall to stall, haggling over the cost of things.

"Good afternoon, Mama."

Doja had found his way through the crowded market to the old woman's stall; his mother's favourite. The old woman was also delighted to see him. It had been long she ever saw Doja at the market. She wondered what winds had blown such an unexpected visit.

"Good afternoon, my son. How is your mother?"

"She is healthy. Please, I need to buy some okra." Doja retorts.

Quickly, he selects the okras he wanted. The patient, old woman now looked at him all over. Doja had grown bigger then she thought. The low moustache strewn across his chin seemed to amaze her too.

"You have grown so big."

The old woman cuts in with her dwindling voice. Doja simply smiles. She teases; pointing towards his chin. This was accompanied by a short-lived laughter. She clasps her fingers against her bony chest, and kept staring at Doja. Doja gave the money to her. She declined at first, but Doja persuades her to. He wasn't surprised when she hands over more than the required quantity to him. Doja thanked her profusely.

Doja was pushing his way out of the market through the milling crowd, when he caught sight of a familiar face. It was a young lady. She had seen him too. And she was waiting with a big smile. He tried to remember her name, as he advanced towards her.

"Jomi, is this really you am seeing?" Doja blurted out, as he stopped in front of her.

Doja could vividly recollect Jomi and he had been childhood friends. They were fond of each other. Sharing and disputing was significant with both. And the whole village used to tease the two children as being a married couple. Their childhood friendship was cut short when Jomi's father died in a sudden mishap. Jomi's mother could not withstand the trauma all by herself. One night, she packed all her belongings, with her children, and left for her father's house at Kajola village. The childhood friends were not allowed to bid each other goodbye.

Doja now admired her all over. She had really changed with time. Jomi was now of average height. Slim, with her dark satin-skin glowing under the afternoon sunlight. Two, tender mounds of flesh over her chest drew Doja's mouth agape. Her well-defined hips complemented the striking figure hidden beneath her resplendent dress. Doja's eyes trailed from her neatly braided hair to her spotless dark toes. His eyes glittered with sparkles of surprise.

"Yes it's me." She replied with delight.

Doja was mesmerized by her white dentition, which dazzled behind her succulent, pinkish lips. Lost in the hypnotism of her matchless beauty, he had faintly heard her response. Little did he know that he had grown into an admirable young man too? Tall, broad-chest, and neatly built. With a remarkable countenance tapered with proportionate hairs around his face. She was also stunned by his appearance.

"You have really changed." Doja teased, after leading her out of the market square, to a cosy place, underneath a mahogany tree at the entrance of the market.

"Same with you," she replied softly.

From her response, Doja could see she hadn't changed. She had always been caring, friendly, and soft-spoken. They stared at each other for a while. Their eyes gleamed with a tingling sensation. Doja could tell he still had a soft spot for Jomi. Even though it's been many years since they parted ways, the sparkles in her brown eyes could tell him she felt the same way about him. They moved closer to each other, and had a long chat.

Doja's late arrival back home was much expected. Amope and Debisi knew their guess had become true, when Doja failed to show up on time. Mother and daughter shared banters and teased one another over who the unknown bride was. Debisi was preparing a yam flour meal, when Doja entered the hut. Debisi grunted in mockery, and Amope threw a dirty glance at her. Amope smiled at her son, as he joined them at the backyard. Amope could see the brightness in his eyes, as he gave her the okras. But she did not say a word about it. Rather, she began humming some marital tunes to herself. She bubbled with joy, believing the gods were finally answering her prayers. She believed her son would bring a wife to the house soon. She praised her ancestors, silently.

The backyard had remained silent for quite some time, before Doja eventually broke the silence. He had much to tell his mother about his reunion with Jomi. Debisi busied preparing the meal, and would not interfere in their conversation.

"Mother, where is Okiki?" Doja started.

"Okiki is sleeping in the hut. Why did you ask?" Amope queried.

"Mother, I met Jomi at the market today." He retorted.

Amope rolled her eyes over. She tried to recollect who Jomi was. But Doja was quick to refresh her memory. Amope was excited; she had known Jomi to be a good natured girl with proper parenting. If Jomi was the unknown bride, Amope was ready to give her full support to her son's choice. She thought to herself, as she smiled.

But Doja was quick to prove her guesses wrong, when he began to explain to his mother that Jomi was now an enlightened person. She had gone to school. And she had learnt the western culture. Amope was surprised to hear this. She shifted from side to side on her stool; eager to hear more. Doja explained further that Jomi told him she received her first level of education from the primary school in Kajola village, where she lived. And she had also gone to the city to further her secondary education. Now that she had graduated from school, she would be returning to the city soon to start a white-collar job.

Amope's jaws dropped, as she listened with rapt attention. Amope knew how excited everyone in her village felt whenever a literate person from the city visited. They would give a long stare and wonder how that person had managed to learn the white man's ways. Even, Debisi who had finished cooking was now curious to hear more.

"Mother, let us send Okiki to school."

Doja's suggestion caught Amope unawares. It was like a gusting wind, blowing at the speed of a gasping messenger. The winds of illumination tore through her whole being. She could not imagine her little son receiving the western education. To Amope, it seemed to be a journey of a lifetime. The thoughts rendered her speechless. Doja, seeing that she was lost in the labyrinth, he expatiated.

"If we send Okiki to school, he would bring us out of ignorance. He would bring the western light to our village. Someday, he would also work in the city. And I believe he would do great."

Amope marvelled, as Doja poured words out of his bottomless well of wisdom. She had always had the feeling that her last child was a symbol of freedom. But the humps would not allow the hunchback to climb the palm-wine tree. Amope began to think about their limitations.

"Don't you think that knowledge would be too difficult for Okiki to grasp?" Amope queried, humbly.

"Mother, a lifetime of ignorance cannot be equated with a lifetime of knowledge." Doja retorted quickly.

Doja's response struck her. She looked into her son's eyes, and could now understand what that brightness she had seen earlier in his eyes when he returned back from the market stood for.

"But we do not have a school in our village. Moreover, no child has ever received western education in this village." She queried further.

"That is why I have called you. You must convince Okiki to accept schooling. He must be the first to receive the western education in this village."

Doja's response proved his determination. Amope sighed. She found it hard to agree. Going to school in the next village, would mean Okiki would have to cover two kilometres by foot, to and fro. That was too much for her dear child. She held her peace. Amope begged for some time to think over the proposal. Doja persuaded that her conclusion should home true his desires for Okiki. While he planned to meet Jomi again, in three days time, in order to get details on how Okiki could start schooling.

As days rolled into nights, Jomi found it hard to forget her encounter with Doja. She daydreamed over their childhood relationship. The good memories flushed rivers of smile over her face. She radiated with joy. Even her siblings wondered what brought a sudden change on her attitude. Nothing could quench her feelings for her lost-and-found childhood friend. She anticipated their next meeting.

The same wind of love had blown over Doja too. Fond memories about Jomi made his heart warm. She was such a pretty angel, as a little girl. But now as a young adult, she was such a sight for sore eyes. Doja couldn't help but think about the lady who had become a perfect example of 'beauty with brain'. Doja watched as the sun rose and went down each day, till that morning they had planned to meet each other again. He wasn't only eager to see her again; he was ready to express his feelings towards her. He set out, that day.

While Doja was away, Amope gave the matter a candid thought. Debisi had also considered her elder brother's intention a wise decision. And she had advised her mother to support the dream. Amope could not resist Doja's opinion either. He was the spearhead of the house. He protected them against the rash conflagrations that aimed towards burning the happiness in their home. His decision could not be underestimated. She believed he must have seen a glorious future in this dream. And she would not stand in his way.

There was a lot for her to think about Okiki too: The child born to her during her trying times. He was her beloved child. She knew him to be a quiet and submissive child. He was a boy with few words in the mouth. He found solace in solitude. And he was contented with everything he got. Amope suddenly realized that she hardly knew what went on in his mind. She knew he was also unhappy with the way things went on in the family, but had barely expressed his feelings. She decided to talk to him.

"Okiki," she called.

Okiki heard at once. He would not mistake his mother's voice for anything else. He searched around the hut. And he found her waiting in her room. Debisi had gone to the market. Adigun was nowhere near home. Okiki found his mother in an unusual mood. It was a mood that held no predictions. The last time she spoke to him in such a mood, was the day she warned him against bed-wetting. He wondered where he had gone wrong this time.

"Am here, mother," he replied timidly.

She gestured, and he sat opposite her. Amope smiled. She did this, whenever she took a deeper look at Okiki. He had resembled both parents. The deep set of eyes, oval face and the round lips, were his mother's. He took his father's erect ears, crowded eyebrows and flat nose. He was such a perfect combination. Above all, he was a handsome little boy.

"Okiki, look into the future, what do you see?" Amope asked candidly, looking at Okiki straight in the eye.

His mother's request shocked him. He wasn't expecting to hear such a question from anyone, not even his mother. But he could not lie; neither could he avoid her question. He cast an unmitigated glance at everything that made up his world. He thought about the incessant hassling from his father; the torturing: angry looks. Worst of all was his mother's unending tears. Okiki felt disillusioned. He was not proud of what he wanted to say. But he would not lie. Not to his mother.

"Tears, mother. Tears" He replied faintly.

Amope was stunned. The boy's response made her feel like a failure. She was not proud of herself. This was not the kind of home she wanted to build. That was not the way she began with her husband; things just suddenly went sour. And she just couldn't help it. She could see that her little boy's mind had already been affected. She now realized what Doja was seeing. Amope knew the innocent boy didn't have to grow up with such thoughts crowded in his mind. She had to create a new path for him. He must find his own destiny. And she hoped the western education would truly be his guiding light.

"Son, there is a way out." She retorted, after a little silence between them.

"Really," Okiki asked brightly.

The little boy, who had been gazing at the gecko on the wall before, now found the nerves to look into his mother's eyes. He felt elated. His home was such a conundrum. He was ready to give all it takes to walk out of such bitterness.

"Yes, my son. You will go to school." She replied again.

Amope could see the puzzle in his eyes. She began to tell him all she knew about schooling. Okiki listened with rapt attention as his mother told him the western education was a cure for ignorance, and a tool for finding solutions to public and personal problems, and ultimately, a key to unlocking one's potentials and fulfilling one's dreams. She told him how much she admired people who visited them from the city, and she had picked all these qualities from them. And now, she certainly believed her last child could become like them someday.

"You will become great. If only you would give your body, your heart and your soul to it." She concluded.

Okiki's mental coast began to enlarge. He swam in his mother's words. He imagined himself being wealthy, powerful and knowledgeable. There was nothing like it. Soon, all their sorrows would be gone. He saw all his bitterness withering at night, and the morning bringing him glorious expectations. He had always wanted to help his mother. And he realised this was his opportunity to do so. He felt delighted.

"I will sacrifice my body, my heart and my soul." He promised.

Amope was glad. She flung her hands wide. And Okiki ran into her embrace. Amope assured Okiki that Doja had gone out for the same purpose. And she was undoubtedly convinced that he would return with optimistic news.

A myriad of revelations dashed across Doja's mind as he raced to the market square. Doja found Jomi already waiting under the mahogany tree. On catching a glimpse of her, a contagious goose-pimple spread over his skin. He shuddered with passion. Jomi was also right in time to catch a glimpse of him. She broke into a smile.

"Am sorry for keeping you await." He said.

"Follow me."

She shushed him affectionately. He kept quiet and followed her meekly. She led the way towards her village. She later broke away from the main route and made a turning to the right. The deserted path was irresolute in its destination. But it was livened by the chirping birds and the rustling rodents. Doja cared less about the flicker of mystery that awaited him. He was hypnotized. He was enraptured by the simultaneous, reverberation of the young lady's waistline. His heart thumped heavily with passion. The path led upwards to the top of a hill.

Suddenly, she stopped. A new world evoked before Doja. The hill was sparsely carpeted with tender grasses. A huge acacia tree stretched its networked branches over the hill. Fully shaded, soft breeze mumbled silently over the hill. From the top of hill, a total view of a gently, sailing stream could be seen far below the hill. The lapping sounds of water gave the vicinity an unparalleled serenity.

Jomi sat down on the soft grass. Doja sat gently beside her. They were silent. The beauty of the place was unconventional. They watched as the water waves unfurled at the base of the hill. The quiescence of the hill brought a whole range of emotions over him. He remained speechless. He racked his brain.

"How did you discover this place?" He whispered.

"I often come here with an intimate friend."

"Is it a male friend or female friend?" Doja demands briskly. Jomi caught a tinge of jealously in his masculine voice. She burst into a hearty peel of laughter. He felt embarrassed.

"Her name is Mary. We both attended the same primary and secondary school."

The word mention of "school" revived the desires of Doja. Jomi threw a full gaze at him. She wondered what the matter was. He turns to her, holding her hands passionately.

"Please, I want my younger brother; Okiki, to receive education."

A surge of desirable emotions transpired between both hands. She felt enthusiastic. He did not let go of the tender hands. He searched through her eyes. He was unable to decipher the language her eyes spoke. His hold seemed to have embroidered her tongue with words unspoken. Her heart began to thump perpetually against her chest. He let go of her hands.

"That's a good intention. When do you want him to commence?" She retorted gleefully. Her response made him feel proud of himself. And he quickly told her he wanted Okiki to enrol in school as soon as possible.

Jomi explained to him that Okiki would first pass through a six year primary education, at the primary school in her village, Kajola. He would then proceed for another six year secondary education in a secondary school in the city. After that, he can choose to get a white-collar job, or precede to the University for a Four year Specialty Program. Doja's mind was spurred as she spoke; he could imagine the amount of knowledge and how great his younger brother would become if he could have all these education.

She continued by telling him that primary education was free at Kajola village because the school belonged to the Missionaries. The only thing he needed to pay for was his school uniforms. And he must come along with a chalk and a slate, as his writing materials. Doja was also pleased to hear that a new session would begin in exactly two weeks time.

"Thank you so much."

Doja thanked her. He was pleased with the procedures. He knew the ball was left in Okiki's court, as he was ready to cater for his education. Doja marvelled at Jomi's motherly gesture, when she volunteered to assist Okiki on the resumption day by leading him to the school and also putting him through the registration procedures. Doja felt satiated. Jomi was certainly the type of woman his mother desired.

The silent hill was such a love-nest. It was a cosy place for two. Doja felt homely. Quiet. Yet, angelic rhythms seemed to tickle their ears. They avoided looking at each other.

"So long . . ." Jomi whispered.

"How yesterday flies . . ." He whispered back.

Slowly, he leans a hand on hers. She shrugs off, affectionately. She stands up and moves towards the edge of the hill. Carefully, folding her arms below her breasts, she stared at her reflection on the stream. Doja lifts himself off the ground sluggishly. And he moved closer to her.

If anyone understood Adigun most, it was his family. Adigun would not play with his farm; a fruitful acre of land, beside the village river. His farm consisted of food crops and cash crops. The unavailability of Okiki, would affect the labour input on his profitable farm. Adigun would never agree to their intention. He was such an adamant and recalcitrant elderly man.

Adigun noticed a slight change in the conduct of his family members when he returned home that evening. They seemed to cluster together, and speak to one another in hushed tones. Their faces showed that they were hiding something. But his paranoid nature told him they were plotting his death. He sniggered, and thought that would be a futile exercise.

"Who will tell father?"

That was what Debisi said after Doja returned home and discussed Okiki's schooling. They were all optimistic and delighted about Okiki receiving the western education. And they felt more encouraged by Okiki's personal interest and enthusiasm. Amope was indeed overjoyed by the new development, but the mention of her husband's name left a sour taste in her mouth. Doja also knew his father would be a cog in their wheel. But he would have to take his chances. He waited for his father to return home.

The gnarled figure leaned on his deck chair, in front of his hut. Wisps of smoke entangled the air surrounding him. He cared less. He huffed and puffed heavily at his pipe. He seemed to enjoy the fragrance from the pipe. He watched the sun grow sulky within the wisps of his smoky pipe. He enjoyed the evening solitude. Suddenly, his smoking serenade was interrupted.

"Father, I need to speak with you."

Doja had materialized from behind. He came out of the hut. Amope, Debisi and Okiki had remained at the backyard, wishing silently. Adigun was infuriated. He hadn't requested for an unwanted discussion. Even though Doja was his first child, yet he was a thorn in his flesh. They were always at loggerheads. They differed in opinions and decisions, and his son often opposed his evil intentions. Adigun wished he could clip his son's wings.

"I want to talk about Okiki." Doja added.

He gave a quick glance at him. Doja could see his father's eyes belching fire. But he was unruffled. Adigun grunted. The name he mentioned didn't seem to prop anything in his mind. Okiki seemed to bore him. Adigun found his last child, unnecessarily docile. He regarded him as a spineless child tied to his mother's apron strings. He found him artless in farming. And he often saw him as a child who would make a mess of his life.

A discussion over Okiki would be similar to collecting a heavy rain with a basket. It was worthless. Adigun piped on. He did not respond. Doja was not bothered by his father's nonchalant attitude. He spoke aloud.

"I want Okiki to start attending school."

"What!" Adigun exclaimed.

Adigun roughly repositioned himself on his chair. Doja reiterated what he said. Adigun's thoughts travelled quickly into his means of livelihood; his farm. Okiki's absence would amount to a loss of labourer. Moreover, Adigun saw the western education as a means of keeping children away from farm. He resented it.

"Okiki would do no such thing!" Adigun bellowed.

"I have promised to cater for his schooling. And I will also add his portion of work on the farm to mine whenever he is away at school." Doja's voice remained calm, as he responded.

Adigun was bewildered by his response. He saw that the plan had already been well thought out. His existence in the family was almost becoming negligible, just as his opinion was almost becoming irrelevant too. He hemmed and hawed before eventually speaking.

"I see Amope's hands in this." Adigun hollered.

"Don't involve mother into this." Doja snapped back.

Adigun stood up. He was livid with anger. But he could also see the look in his son's eyes was defiant and filled with rage too. Adigun knew it was now becoming pertinent for him to do something about his son's defiance and disregard towards him. He murmured something threatening and stormed away.

Doja caught the challenge. He was undaunted. His position was sacrosanct. There would be no turning back. Once the monitor-lizard jumps down from a tree, it bolts away.

— 4 —

A Child of Destiny

H E HAD WOKEN up before the first cock crow. Amope thought he was still fast asleep when she woke him up. But Okiki had hardly slept throughout the night. His mind wandered about what his first day at school would be like.

His mind was lost in his first visitation to the Missionary school. That was a week ago. Okiki had followed Jomi meekly to the school for his enrolment. He could remember staring at the blocks of classrooms. His eyes had wandered around the big school compound beautifully strewn with variegated flowers. His eyes clearly moved from one thing to the other, as Jomi led him.

But mostly, his ears were stunned by words he could barely pronounce or remember. He smiled as the language made beautiful words in his ears. And he wished he could synchronise his lips along as Jomi spoke the foreign language with the administrative officers. He knew that was the western language. It was called English. And he knew that was one of the benefits of education; he would speak like a British. Okiki was really glad he had been enrolled in school. His mind told him he truly belonged there.

Okiki set forth at dawn. He walked as fast as his legs could carry him. His writing slate and chalks were firmly placed in the school sack slashed across his neck. He could hardly hear the birds chirping. He remembered his dear mother as he walked along the lonely footpath. Some minutes back he had left her, and he could see the deep concern in her eyes. She had quietly helped him to pack his school writing materials, and keep a few bean cakes he could eat at school, in his school sack. She did not say a word to him, as he walked out of the hut. But he could hear her heart thumping loud in his ears. A heart that was bleeding love: telling him to remember the son of whom he was.

"What would you do if you had a chance to decide your fate?"

Okiki had almost passed the old tree when he heard the voice of the cashew tree. A tinge of guilt ran down his spine. It's been weeks since he visited the wise, old tree. He had even failed to tell his mysterious friend about his schooling pursuit. Worst of all, his mind was engrossed to the point that he took no notice of the significant object by the path.

"Good morning." Okiki greeted, pretending not to hear what the mysterious tree had said.

"What would you do if you were left alone in this world?" The cashew tree rephrased.

Okiki was too young to comprehend the question. He barely knew anything. And he knew from his little interaction with the mysterious tree, its wisdom was unfathomable. He kept quiet, and waited for the mysterious tree to give him the right response. The cashew tree read Okiki's mind, and felt impressed by the innocent boy's wise decision.

"Opportunity has presented itself before your footsteps, use it wisely. Education is like a magic wand: swing it and you will find answers to all you ever dreamed of. Okiki, you are a child of destiny. You are alone in this world, as the fates of others depend on yours. There will be many storms ahead, but always return to your centre: your inner being. And always remember that you have all it takes to succeed."

Okiki listened with rapt attention. The mysterious tree had always spoken to him succinctly; but that morning was different. He carefully kept the words in the heart of his heart, where nothing could erode it from his thoughts. He sighed loudly, and thanked his mysterious friend.

"Your life is a gift. Do not waste it." He could hear the mysterious tree's final words as he hurried off to school.

Amope was at the backyard washing when she heard some rustling sounds at the front of the compound. It had been hours since her husband and her children left for the farm. She was not expecting anyone. She removed her wet hands from the dishes, and went to check who or what it was. Amope was surprised to see Adigun waiting at the entrance of the hut. His eyes were blazing with fury. Amope could see his countenance and she could also see he was also holding a cutlass in his hand.

She withdrew her steps before she could even think of asking her husband why he had come. Adigun was infuriated by her movement; thinking she already knew why he was angry with her. He suddenly dropped the cutlass and gave her a hot chase. Amope recoiled and ran for safety. But Adigun was too fast for her; he caught up with her as she tried escaping through the back door. He struck her heavily with the back of his hand, and Amope hit her face against the door post. She lost control and fell down. Adigun fiercely kicked her all over. Amope cried and screamed for help. But no one heard.

"You foolish woman, despite my warnings, you and your bastard son decided to send Okiki to school. We shall see who laughs last." Adigun bellowed, raining expletives on his wife, as he stormed out of the hut.

Okiki was the first person to return back to the hut later that afternoon. He was coming back home with so much excitement. And he had a lot of interesting incidents he wanted to share with his family. Amope had heard the footsteps of her little child in the compound, and she had rushed out to welcome him. Minutes after her husband left, she had washed her face and dried her tears. Amope was careful not to leave any trace for her children to see. But Okiki's excitement waned, and the smile on his face disappeared as soon as his mother materialized. He could see a dark circle around his mother's left eye. Amope had a black eye.

"Mother, what happened to your eye," Okiki cried, pointing at the eye.

Amope was taken aback. She had observed that her left eye was hurting when she was washing her face. She could remember she had hit it against the door post when her husband attacked her. But she did not know that blood clotting had formed dark circles around her eye. She quickly thought of what to say.

"I hit it against the wooden pillar at the cooking shed." She lied.

Okiki traced her eyes, and he knew his mother had lied. He gave a weak smile, and asked her if it didn't hurt much. Amope replied calmly, thinking her little son did not understand a thing.

"Mother, let me tell you what happened at school today," Okiki burst out, when they got inside.

"Wait, eat your food first. You will tell us when your siblings return." Amope teased.

Doja and Debisi returned home a few hours after. Okiki and Amope were excited to see them. They were equally eager to return home too, since they knew Okiki would have a lot to tell them. Okiki sprang up and ran to welcome them. Adigun had veered off on the way, and left to see his friends. So they knew they would have ample time to chat loudly and laugh hilariously.

Debisi was the first to enter the hut, and she had seen her mother's black eye. But she was yet to fully comprehend what went wrong. Doja was about to enter the hut, when he saw an old cutlass by the entrance. The cutlass was familiar. The cutlass had history. He could not mistake his father's cutlass for anything else. He bent down and picked it up. Hours back, Amope had been thinking of what to tell her first son. She knew he would certainly not believe the lie she told Okiki. Seeing Doja pick up the cutlass, Amope knew her cover had been blown.

"Doja, come," Amope called him boldly.

Doja looked forward and saw his mother. He also saw the black eye. Anger welled up in his mind. He knew there was no amount of lie she could tell him, this was his father's doing. He held his breath, and complied.

Amope led Doja to the backyard, far from where the other two children could eavesdrop and hear their conversation. She knelt down before her son, and begged him not to take offence by his father's misdeed. Doja's angered quickly melted away, when he saw his mother kneeling before him. He quickly pulled her to her feet, and told her he would overlook the matter, if only she told him why she had been mercilessly beaten up by his irate father.

"It was because of Okiki." She replied.

Doja felt embittered towards his father. He was the one that had initiated and sponsored Okiki's education. He wondered why his father could be so unreasonable. And he wondered why he was such a coward, by transferring his aggression on his helpless mother. He sighed deeply, holding back his anger.

"Should we stop Okiki's schooling?" Doja enquired.

"No!" Amope retorted.

Amope knew Adigun had done his worst. There was nothing more he could do. His action was just a verisimilitude of a snake that had been hacked with a machete. Doja held his mother in a long embrace, and thanked her for her perseverance.

Okiki was already talking to his sister about his first day at school when Amope and Doja returned into the hut. They sat quietly and joined the conversation.

" . . . even my class-teacher's chair is better than father's 'pipe-smoking' chair." Okiki remarked in low tones. They all burst into wild laughter; knowing he was talking about Adigun's deck chair. Adigun had held the wooden chair in such a high esteem; his father had given him. And he would not allow any of his children touch it, talk less of sitting on it. Adigun relished lying on the chair, and smoking tobacco with his smoking-pipe.

"But mother, I was given a new name," Okiki cuts in.

"A new name," they all chorused, even though he had directed the speech at his mother.

They all listened as Okiki told them his native name was condemned by the Missionary school's Priest, and he was given a new name. Okiki told them the Priest; a white man had told him his name was dedicated to a pagan god. Debisi cuts in; asking if the Priest really had a white skin. Amope and Doja gave her a queer look. But Okiki was quick to respond telling her that the Priest had a pale complexion; almost white. And he was quick to add that they were often referred to as being 'white' because they came from a superior race.

"So what name were you given?" Amope asks impatiently. Eager to know which name had been given to her little child.

"Joseph," he replied.

They all chorused the name, slurring it. Okiki told them the Priest had given him an English name. A name drawn from the western religion, called Christianity.

"I hope the name has a rich and positive meaning like the one we gave you?" Amope enquired. The native woman agreed the British were superior to them in every way, but she seemed to disagree with the changing of name; because her little boy's name meant 'Fame' as he was shortly called. The full pronunciation of the name was 'Okikioluwa' which simply meant 'God's fame.' Okiki also knew he came from a tribe which believed that a child's name has a lot to do with their destiny; as such he knew he had to find out what the name 'Joseph' meant.

The next time Doja saw Jomi, he was supposed to ask what Okiki's foreign name meant, but he had been enraptured by a beauty that had no equal. The two lovers now seemed to bind together just the way a snail cannot detach from its shell. They rekindled the flame of love that existed between them, and they could easily see that they shared a lot of things in common. As Doja stared at the stream below the hill, sailing gently, he knew sometime soon he and Jomi would tread the journey of life together, as one.

Okiki soared in knowledge as he became the talk of the village. Whenever he was returning from school he would be stopped by one or two villagers who often admired his brown, khaki school uniform, and they wanted to know what he was learning at school. What gave him concern most was the traders at Kajola market; he always had to pass through the market every schooling day, and he had become a centre of attraction for the market women.

"Okiki what did you learn today?" they would ask, whenever he returned from school.

"Many things," he would reply.

The word 'many' made their ignorant minds wander about a lot of things. They knew the Europeans were full of knowledge, and for one of their sons to grasp such knowledge must have been a herculean task. Truly, they believed Okiki would have to learn many things, if he wished to have a 'white-brain'. They all admired him, enviously. But they did not know that Okiki was still learning how to write the English alphabets.

— 5 —

The Strange Sickness

THAT AFTERNOON, OKIKI was full of joy. He had been promoted to the next class. Education had become a great delight to him. He was proud to be acquiring knowledge beyond the seas and shores of his fatherland. He was happy he had not been a disappointment to his elder brother. And he was sure his mother's hope would be rekindled with this success. He stopped by the cashew tree, to have a little chat before going home that afternoon.

"I have been promoted to the next class," Okiki bursts out, gleefully.

"I am so happy for you. But can I ask you a question?" The cashew tree retorts.

"Go ahead."

"What would you do with all the knowledge you acquire?" The mysterious tree asks.

Okiki kept quiet. And he had to think about the cashew tree's question carefully. He had often thought his education was all about him and his family. But his instincts now told him he was made for something more. Something beyond his own: A dream that reflected upon the liberation of his people.

"I want to save my people." He replied, thoughtfully.

"Good. But do you know that you have to save yourself first?" The Cashew tree asked further.

Okiki knew he had no answer. He wasn't quite sure if he needed to be saved, or how to be saved. He had wanted to ask the mysterious tree how he would know if he needed to be saved or not, when the cashew tree continued,

"You are just a reflection of your environment. You need to poise yourself for leadership, by always being at the centre of all the situations surrounding and affecting you. Be the change you want to see."

Okiki leaned his back against the cashew tree, and took a deep breath. He just couldn't fathom the depth of the mysterious tree's wisdom. He thought about the solution the cashew tree proffered. Truly, the vices in his village were caused by a few people who could not control their desires; hence they affected a whole lot of people. And likewise, the virtues shared amongst his people were sustained by a few who could control their desires. Okiki took this as a great learning, and he seemed ready to conquer the future.

"Run! Run!! Save your mother!!!"

Okiki was shocked by the cashew tree's exclamation. In the little while he had known the mysterious tree, one attribute that made the whole difference was that the cashew tree was omniscient. He wondered what must have been happening to his beloved mother. He sprang to his feet and sped towards his home.

Debisi approached the hut from a corner with a big pot on her head. She was coming from the village river. That was her third round going to and from the river. She had filled most of the empty containers, and the one she was carrying inside the hut ought to be the last. Adigun was sitting on his deck chair in front of the hut, smoking tobacco. He often stayed at home nowadays since the planting season was over. Doja too was equally free from farm work, and he had gone out to visit his friends.

Amope had just finished preparing lunch. She was waiting for Okiki to return from school. Suddenly she felt heat stoke within her belly, she started feeling feverish. She gripped her head. Debisi was already offloading the pot on her head, when she caught sight of her mother's strange behaviour. She quickly let down the pot, and hurried towards her mother. Amope's body suddenly stiffened. Her whole body twirled on one foot, and she slammed her body against the hard floor.

"Father" Debisi screamed.

She ran to the front of the hut, and sought her father's assistance. Adigun had heard her call. He peeped into the hut, and saw his wife rolling violently on the harsh floor. He hissed and concentrated on smoking his pipe. Debisi ran towards her father in tears; begging him to show some concern and offer some assistance. Adigun did not budge. Debisi ran back inside, panting.

Doja had seen his younger sister run back inside the hut, as he approached the hut from a far distance. He could sense something was wrong. He ran as fast as he could. Debisi was gasping and crying, when Doja ran past his father and hurried inside. The two siblings watched helplessly, as their mother's body became taut, with bulging eyes. They had not even noticed Okiki run into the hut, until he screamed,

"Mother"

Okiki rushed forward to rescue his dying mother. Doja grabbed him before he could get near her. Okiki wailed and struggled to be free as he saw his mother writhing in pains. Doja held him firmly in a strong embrace. He begged Okiki to remain calm, but his words landed on deaf ears. Amope's violent movements waned, and she began foaming at the mouth. Okiki couldn't bear watching the mass of white bubbles around his mother's mouth. He continued screaming and struggling to be free from his brother's grip. Debisi was also in tears, and she was begging for mercy from the gods. But she did not move near her mother either. Doja pulled all his inner strength to fight back the tears. Amope was helpless, her children watched her in pity.

After a short while, Amope lay still. She had become pale. Okiki screamed loudly again, thinking his mother had become lifeless. But Doja did not let him go. A cool breeze blew across the hut, and Amope opened her eyes. Debisi and Okiki stopped crying, and the hut became silent. Amope had become rough and dirty. She struggled to sit up, and Debisi hurried closely to help her. Doja let go of Okiki, but Okiki had become numb by the short experience that seemed to have lasted for a lifetime. Okiki sank to the ground, and sat, staring at his mother. Doja and Debisi helped her to her feet. They led her to the bathroom, and returned shortly.

Debisi disappeared to the backyard, and returned with some soft sands. Okiki watched as his sister scattered the sands over the sputum on the floor. Doja went to the front of the hut, and Adigun was nowhere to be found. He was even nowhere near the hut. He had left a long time, while Amope was still passing through her epilepsy fit.

Amope returned back to the main hut, bathed, refreshed, and in new clothes. But her look was depressed. Her body ached, but she managed to force a weak smile. Okiki could see the bruises around her face and body, but he did not say a word. Misery gnawed at his peace of mind. He was too distraught to say a word. He had heard whispers about his mother's strange sickness. But he just couldn't bear witnessing the whole scene. It was such a huge trauma for the little child.

The sun had set. And the hut was getting dark. Debisi appeared with a bowl of boiled water and a piece of cloth. Doja had remained outside the hut. But the evening breeze could not cool his anger towards his father. Amope sat firmly on a wooden stool. Okiki watched as Debisi dipped the fabric into the hot water; squeeze it a little, and rub it gently over Amope's bruised areas. Amope whined like a baby.

The atmosphere in the room was sullen and emotional. Debisi and Okiki felt pity for their mother. But they chose not to say a word. The words would have been empty and meaningless. Instead, they wept silently.

"Come, my son." Amope beckoned at Okiki.

Her voice was weary and dry. Debisi had finished massaging her mother's bruises. She sat quietly at a dark corner, and watched as Okiki crawled towards his mother. Doja too had returned into the hut, to see how their mother was faring. Okiki sat beside his mother, not saying a word. He averted his eyes.

"How was school today?" Amope asked.

Okiki wanted to lie. His spirit was in melancholy. And he found no reason to tell his mother the joyous news. At that moment, his success felt meaningless to him. His mother's happiness was paramount. But he did not lie.

"I have been promoted to the next class." He replied, weakly.

Amope's face lit with surprise. It seemed a butterfly flew across her mind. She broke into a wide smile. Debisi and Doja had also heard Okiki; they could not hide their joy. They also broke into a brilliant smile. Amope was joyous; she did not know the exact words to express how she felt. She pulled her little boy into an embrace, and hugged him for as long as she could remember. Doja and Debisi felt proud of their little brother. They moved closer, and hugged him too. Amope looked into Okiki's eyes and said,

"You will wipe away my tears. You will bring me a lasting joy."

The words made Okiki shiver all over. His feelings soared, but he was still embittered about his mother's health crisis. Okiki broke into a fresh round of tears, hugging his mother tightly, and hiding his face in her bosom. Amope caressed his hair, and wished him well silently.

Debisi laid down the mat and Amope went inside to sleep. She needed a lot of rest that day, and even in the subsequent days that followed. Okiki followed, and had declined from eating his supper that day. He slept quietly beside his mother. Debisi tidied up every other duty, while Doja waited for his father.

Okiki was awakened at night, by a loud noise coming from the compound. It was an altercation between Doja and their father. Amope was sound asleep; she did not hear a word. Even Debisi who had been spent during the day's chores was sound asleep, and snoring. Okiki carefully crawled away from his mother's side towards the door. So that he could have a clearer view of what was going on.

"Father, why are you so heartless?" Doja challenged.

"What do you mean?" Adigun retorted, half-drunk.

"Why do you hate mother so much?"

"You are a fool!" Adigun barked.

"Father, why don't you care about our feelings?" Doja pressed further, ignoring Adigun's earlier remark.

"You must be insane!" Adigun snapped back, raising his hand up to slap Doja. Doja seized his hand mid-air. Adigun was shocked.

"You must be cursed." Adigun hollered.

"Father, I am not," Doja snapped back, he was now livid with anger, "and don't ever lay your hands upon mother again!"

"You have been cursed!" Adigun barked again, as Doja disappeared into the night. That was the first time Doja refused to sleep inside the hut.

Adigun knew his days were numbered. His son's audacity was growing beyond measure. Home was becoming unbearable for him. Hating his wife had become a habit, and he knew it. Kasali, his bosom friend had helped him secure a secret concubine from one of the neighbouring villages. He had once lingered over the choice, but now, there was no going back. Not only would he marry a second wife, he would also escape with her.

But Doja did not dwell much of the following days thinking about his father's intolerance. He rather thought about his beauty goddess; Jomi. She had informed him earlier that she would be leaving for the city in a few days time, and he worried about the long days ahead. They had both rejoiced when she informed him that she received an employment letter for a lucrative white-collar job in the city. But shortly after, he started feeling uncertain if she would not forget him in the village, and abandon him for an educated guy in the city.

"You don't have to be worried, Doja?" Jomi said, standing in front of him. Doja did not reply. He just kept staring at her. Now that their love was blossoming, it would be too early to create such distances.

The sparkles in her eyes that day did assure him that her heart was with him, and would always be. Jomi even suggested Doja should come and live with him in the city, but he resented the idea. Doja understood that leaving his family under the present condition is like sleeping in a house with a burning roof. He needed to stay by his mother, and help Okiki achieve his academic dreams. Jomi did understand his plight, and she promised to always pay him a visit whenever she had the opportunity to do so.

"The days ahead may be lonely, but be sure that my heart would always be with you." Jomi stressed, holding Doja close to her heart.

Still, he did not say a word. That evening was the last day he was going to see her before she leaves for the city at dawn by lorry. His mind raced across many things. He was speechless. Seeing that he remained mute, Jomi withdrew away from him and faced another direction. The two lovers became silent.

The evening was still and serene under the sunlight. Butterflies flitted from flowers to flowers. And the two hearts breathed heavily under the momentarily thoughts of distance. Jomi knew she was going to miss him. She loved him with so much innocence and passion. And she knew he loved her too. But some things were not meant to be hurried. If only he would understand, if only he would allow her to take the lead. She wanted him to let her explore the opportunities available to her, so that together they can build a decent and enviable family. She wished he understood.

Doja had heard her wishes, as he stood watching her back. He had known her for quite some time now, and he knew she was incapable of acting without thinking deeply about it. Jomi was an intelligent young lady, and he respected her like his mother. Gently, he walked towards her, and hugged her from behind. She also responded back by holding the arms wrapped around her.

"I will wait for you." He whispered into her ears.

"I will wait for you too." She whispered back.

During the long holiday, Okiki spent most of his hours revising all he had learnt in his first session at school. Amope watched her little son closely, and was impressed by his persistent desire to acquire the western knowledge. She once feared the knowledge may break down his memory, but now she could see that all that was needed was an open heart and a strong will. Okiki had these virtues, and Amope knew he was destined for great things.

Okiki still did not lag in his home chores and farming responsibilities. He helped his mother with the house chores, and he also supported his elder brother at the farm. Debisi enjoyed chatting with her younger brother, and since he was on holiday, Okiki did not deprive her of the opportunity whenever they were less busy at home. But mostly, Okiki preferred speaking with the cashew tree. He willing learnt his ears unto the wisdom coming from the lips of the mysterious tree. Okiki was careful enough to know when to visit the cashew tree, since the tree was by the path to the village market.

That afternoon, Okiki knew the path to the market would be deserted. So he ventured to visit his mysterious friend. He had a lot to discuss with the cashew tree, but mostly, he wanted to talk about his mother's illness. And he had also wanted to talk about his father too. Suddenly, he stopped. The little boy could hear silent whispers coming from a nearby farm. One of the voices was familiar. Okiki stopped and peered closer to see who they were.

"Don't tell me that's an easy thing to do," the young woman said.

"But it is," the man replied.

"What exactly are your plans for me?" She pressed further.

"I am going to make you my wife," the man retorted briskly.

"What about your wife?" She snapped back.

"There is nothing she can do."

"Tell me more," she persisted, and the man drew closer to her, and whispered some words into her ears.

Her expression changed, and she smiled coyly. The man ran his fingers through her braided hair and caressed it. The lady blushed and snuggled closer to feel the warmth on his chest. Okiki had seen the young woman in a multicoloured blouse, but he could hardly see the face of the man until he drew closer to her. Okiki was stultified to see that the man she was speaking with was his father!

He held his breath, and quietly sneaked away from the spot without being noticed. Once far from the scene, the innocent boy took to his heels and ran. He ran without compulsion. He ran to turn back the hands of time, he wished he had not seen or heard a thing. His heart was broken. He ran to melt away his fears.

"So what are you going to do?" The cashew tree demanded.

Okiki had stopped in front of the cashew tree. He embraced the tree tightly, to fight back his anger.

"I will challenge him!" Okiki blurted out. And he was surprised to see the cashew tree burst into a hilarious laughter. Okiki became more furious.

"I dislike him! He never makes us happy. What is the relevance of his presence?"

"Quiet!" The cashew tree shushed the little boy.

"You must learn to tread your grounds softly. If you don't, the ground would swallow you." Okiki was silenced by the words of the cashew tree. The little boy was scared by the idea of an earthquake. He calmed down and listened to the cashew tree.

"You don't dip your fingers inside boiling oil; it burns. Listen to your mother, listen to patience."

Okiki felt ashamed of himself. Often times he had misunderstood his mother's patience as an act of cowardice, but now he could see it was a sign of strength and courage. He could now see that his anger would not produce any positive result. He realised that castigating or criticizing his father should not be in his own jurisdiction. He took a deep breath, and made up his mind never to judge the errors of those ahead of him. Rather, he would work hard on becoming a better person, whom others would love to emulate.

The cashew tree was proud of Okiki. He was such an innocent and wise boy. All he needed was a little advice and caution, and those words would metamorphose into a spring of wisdom within him. Okiki thanked the cashew tree for the advice and caution. The little boy returned home that evening with a costly secret hidden in his mind.

6

The Breaking Point

THE FIRST TIME he saw her, he knew there was something different about her. There was something unique and endearing about her. Something that made her stood out as being more important than the teachers that had taught him before.

Mary was Okiki's new class-teacher. All the pupils were astonished when she walked into the class on the resumption day. She was slim, average height, and had a fair skin. Her hair was dark-brown, and her eyebrows neatly cropped above her eyes. She was beautiful. She introduced herself that day as their new class-teacher, and also informed them that she would be their class-teacher throughout their schooling days. The delighted students couldn't wish for more.

But her first encounter with Okiki was not a splendid one. Okiki had dozed off during class. Mary was furious. But she did not express her anger towards him. She simply asked his colleagues to wake him up. Okiki did not wake up until the fifth nudge by the pupil sitting next to him. He felt totally ashamed when he saw that he had drawn so much attention while sleeping. Everyone laughed as he raised his sleepy face up.

"Indeed, you are *Joseph the dreamer*," Mary remarked and there was a great roar of laughter. Okiki was embarrassed. He certainly knew his classmates were as much novice as he was pertaining to the meaning of his English name. But the sarcastic remark made by their class-teacher told a lot about who Joseph must have been, or what the name must have meant. He felt a sudden dislike for the name.

Mary had called Okiki aside that day, during break, and asked why he had slept off during the class. Okiki felt jittery. He did not say a word. He just stared at her. Mary felt he was still ashamed of himself, or probably intimidated, so she let him go.

Okiki felt embittered towards himself that afternoon, on his way home. He blamed himself for sleeping during class. He felt he had made a bad impression of himself before his new class-teacher. But he just couldn't help but rest his head during class that day; the early morning journey from his village to school had always exhausted his energy. And he had always wrestled with himself everyday over a little nap. But he just didn't win that day. He bit his lips. More confusing, was the discovery about his English name. He began to feel probably that was the reason why he often felt sleepy, and eventually slept off in class that day. This was a bad revelation for him. But he would not tell his mother.

That day had also been a displeasing one for Debisi; Okiki's elder sister. Amope had sent her to the market during the day. She had bought the necessary condiments, and was on her way back when she met Kasali; her father's closest companion. Kasali had seen her coming, and was enraptured by her beauty. His eyes had been on Debisi since when she was a teenager. His passion for her was so strong, and he just couldn't help it. Adigun had always been provoked whenever Kasali suggested having his daughter's hands in marriage. But Kasali just could not forego the thought.

"How are you, Debisi?" Kasali's eyes trailed her all over as he greeted her.

"Good afternoon, am fine." She replied briskly, hating the way he looked at her.

"Are you on your way home," he asked foolishly.

"Yes. And I have to hurry along now." She replied quickly, and hurried along.

Kasali remained rooted to the spot, as his eyes trailed Debisi as she walked away. He smiled coyly, knowing it takes a patient dog to eat a fat bone. Debisi fumed with anger as she walked back home. She was matured enough to understand Kasali's advances towards her. She just couldn't imagine herself being married to her father's mate; talk less of becoming a second wife. She kept this thought to herself.

Amope's heart also weighed with so much heaviness. And it was already affecting her relationship with her children. Amope realised that her husband hardly stayed at home, since his altercation with Doja, many months back. Whenever he was at home, he kept to himself. And he hardly ate Amope's food.

Adigun would not eat Amope's food since his secret concubine now fed him special dishes. His intimacy with her blanketed his thoughts, so much he hardly wanted to come home. He was enjoying his moments with this unknown woman. And he was already planning on how to secretly escape with her. Kasali, his friend had discouraged the idea when he told him. Adigun felt he was the one that knew where the shoe was pinching him, and hence, he refused to discuss the issue with his intimate friend anymore.

Okiki took pity on his mother. But he would not say a word. He knew it was the strange woman that made his father stay away from home. But he would not tell his mother. Moreover, his father's absence from home had brought so much peace and tranquillity. But Amope did not feel that way. Her mind equally suggested her husband was having a secret affair, but she gnawed at such flimsy thoughts. She rather thought of how to pacify her husband whenever the opportunity presented itself.

Another opportunity did present itself for Okiki to know his class-teacher better, or probably for her to know him better. This was many weeks after Okiki's embarrassing moment with his new class-teacher. Since that time, he had avoided her eyes, and also stayed out of trouble. Even though his classmates now called him 'Joseph the Dreamer'.

"Who is Okiki in this class?" Mary called out.

Okiki was surprised to hear Mary call him by his native name. He was called Joseph at school, just like all the other students were also called by their English names. Weakly, he rose up a feeble finger. Mary was surprised to know it was him.

"So, it's you Joseph. See me during break time." She said.

Okiki kept wondering what the matter could be. He wondered how his class teacher had known his name. He could not feed on these thoughts much; since the break period was just a few minutes away.

Mary had first made him sit down in front of her. That was one of the things that made Mary different from all the teachers that had taught Okiki. She showed a lot of care and respect for her students. But Okiki did not have the courage to tell her so. He sat down quietly, averting his eyes.

"So, you are the student that comes from the other village?" Mary began.

"Yes, I am." Okiki's voice was thin. Mary barely heard him.

"I am sorry for embarrassing you in class the other day. I guess it was the long journey from your village down to school that made you tired. Please don't be offended by my actions." She apologized.

Okiki could hardly believe his ears. He felt elated by Mary's kind apology. But he did not say a word. He still avoided her eyes, wondering if that was the reason why she had called him.

"I have a letter for Doja," she cuts in.

Immediately he heard his brother's name being mentioned, he looked up and stared at his class-teacher. "How could she have known his elder brother's name?" He thought to himself.

"He has a letter from my friend in the city; Jomi." Mary continued.

Okiki could not believe his ears. He could now find his way out of the whole maze. He could also remember he had seen Jomi talking to Mary, on the day she came to enrol him in school. Definitely, Mary and Jomi were intimate friends. And the latter could have sent the letter to Mary via the school post office box.

Suddenly his mind switched as Mary brought out the letter. The two of them looked at each other's eyes, and burst into an uncontrollably roar of laughter. The letter had shown that Jomi and Doja were in love with each other. The thoughts made them feel mockery for the two love birds. Okiki calmly collected the letter from his class-teacher, thanked her, and left. Mary watched Okiki leave, and she noticed he had a little resemblance with her younger brother who got drowned in the river, many years back. She sighed.

Okiki met his mother and siblings at the backyard when he returned back from school that day. Amope wore a sullen look. Her husband who had left for days was yet to return. The children were less concerned, since they knew his presence spelt trouble. Doja wondered why his mother felt troubled. But Amope would not speak to anyone. The emergence of Okiki in the home livened up their mood. He was special and loved by all of them. They were all eager to know what happened at school.

"Brother, are you expecting any message from someone?" Okiki started, and all eyes turned to Doja who quickly replied in the negative.

"What about a special message from a special friend?" Okiki teased further. Amope and Debisi turned to look at Doja again. His face wore bewilderment. He wondered what Okiki was driving at. He did not reply.

"I mean a special letter from a dear friend." Okiki remarked playfully. Doja's eyes lit up. He now understood what his younger brother was trying to say. Amope and Debisi were taken aback as Doja sprang to his feet and chased Okiki around the compound.

"Give it to me! Give it to me!!" Doja shouted as Okiki ran around laughing and refusing to let go of the letter. Doja caught up with him, and lifted him up in the air. He turned Okiki around in circles, and the little boy yelled. Debisi laughed hilariously as Amope begged Doja to let his brother down.

Doja snatched the letter from Okiki's hands and hurried out of the hut. He felt embarrassed because everyone now understood what the letter meant, and where it came from. Doja had greatly missed Jomi. He missed her with every passing moment. Life seemed boring for him, since she left. He had been expecting a message from her, and he was so excited to finally have her letter in his hands.

"What could she have written inside?" He said to himself as he hurried down to their usual meeting place. He knew that would be the best place to read the letter. His heart was beating fast as he walked.

It was already getting late into the night when a shadowy figure appeared in front of the hut. Doja had not returned since he left the house in the afternoon. But Amope knew the shadow she was seeing did not resemble that of her son. It was more like her husband. Debisi and Okiki were at the backyard preparing supper. Okiki placed fresh logs of firewood in the fire and stoked it. Amope stood up and walked towards the entrance. Adigun staggered into the hut.

Adigun had spent that evening with Kasali at Iya Sadi's palm-wine grove. He had been away with his secret concubine, and had returned to celebrate his final departure with his friend. Even though Kasali did not subscribe to his friend's plan to desert his family. But he would not allow a little difference to damage their long term friendship.

Kasali drank to his friend's departure. Adigun drank towards his eventual freedom and unending bliss. They exchanged banters and laughed loudly. Their hours of condescension passed, and the two friends left the grove heavily drunk. Kasali bid his friend goodbye as Adigun returned to his home to pack a few belongings he would disappear with.

Amope hurriedly went down on her knees begging her husband for any misdemeanour she might have caused, which had led him into disappearing from home for the past few days. Adigun did not even take notice of her. He staggered past her, and went into his room. Amope followed behind, begging him. Debisi and Okiki had heard their mother's plea, and they knew their father was back. But they remained at the backyard. Okiki could sense trouble was looming on the horizon, and he wished his elder brother returned home immediately.

Doja suddenly woke up. He had slept off on the tuft grass after reading Jomi's letter. The content of the letter had played love strings in his ears. It brought a pleasing smile to his face, and warmth settled in his heart. He could also see how much Jomi had missed him, and how much his love burned in her heart. He read the letter over and over again. And he thought visiting his sweetheart in the city wouldn't be such a bad idea after all. He did not know when he dozed off in his romantic imaginations.

Doja sprang to his feet, and hurried down the hill. He hurried through the bush, as the sounds of night crickets ushered him all the way back to his hut.

Amope cried silently, as she watched her husband pack a few things in a bag. She begged him silently, and was afraid to touch him. She thought the other woman's spell was working on him. She knew that if she allowed him to leave that night, he might never come back to the hut again. She stood sentinel against the door.

Adigun finished packing a few things and turned to go out of the room. Seeing his wife blocking his way, he gave her a sullen glare and brushed past her. Amope ran after him and grabbed his foot. Adigun was enraged by her touch. He dragged her along, but Amope did not let go. Her tender skin peeled against the hard floor, and she groaned painfully. Adigun tried to wrestle his leg free, but Amope held it tightly. Adigun was provoked. He swung the other foot, and it hit Amope right in her mouth. The impact was drastic, as her mouth began to bleed. The helpless woman screamed out.

Okiki stirred up in riposte. He and his sister had heard the murmurings in the hut, and had felt it was their parent's usual quarrel. So they stayed away from it. But when they heard their mother's loud scream, they knew the situation was getting beyond control. Okiki ran inside the hut, and Debisi followed speedily. The two children were unhappy to see their mother's face in blood. They rushed to help.

"Okiki, Okiki, get the bag." Amope begged, as she struggled to get to her feet. Okiki took a glance at his father and saw him trying to pick up his bag which had fallen when he recklessly kicked his wife. Debisi wrapped around Amope, and tried to help her away from her irate husband. Okiki was quick enough to grab the bag.

"How dare you!"

Adigun exclaimed and pursued Okiki. The little boy ran aimlessly around the dark hut, and fled towards the backyard. Unfortunately, his legs stumbled on an object, and he fell. Okiki scrambled back to his feet, but Adigun caught up with him and threw a furious punch at the innocent boy. The punch sent Okiki reeling backwards, landing on the hard floor with a loud thud. He became unconscious. Amope and Debisi screamed.

"Okiki"

Debisi rushed towards Okiki, and carried him to a safe corner in the hut. Amope sprang to her feet and ran towards Adigun. She got hold of her husband's cloth, and tried to stop him from leaving. Before Debisi could hurry to stop her mother from the act, the irate man had sent his wife falling backwards with a sharp head-butt. Amope fell luckily into Debisi's hands.

"I will kill you tonight!" Adigun yelled.

The atmosphere in the hut was tepid and dangerous. Debisi could see her father running towards the backyard to pick a harmful object. She tried to help Amope out of harm's way, but the helpless woman was irresolute. Adigun reappeared with a pestle in his hand. The two women screamed and ran for their dear lives. Adigun swung the pestle at Amope, and it caught her by the shoulder blade. Amope yelped and fell down.

"Father, please," Debisi begged.

Adigun was defiant. He lifted the pestle in the air again, and attempted to strike Amope again. The reflection of the moon in the hut was suddenly blocked by a shadowy figure. Adigun took a glance, and before he could see ahead, Doja was already in front of him, and had caught the pestle mid-air. The two men began to struggle over the pestle. Doja smelled his father's breath, and knew he was drunk. He jabbed him lightly on the thigh, and Adigun staggered backwards and lost control of the pestle. Doja had heard the noise coming from his hut from a far distance. And he had sneaked in carefully, before Adigun caught sight of him. Doja knew their neighbours must have heard the noise too, but must have declined from quelling the fight, in order to get out of harm's way.

"Bastard" Adigun hollered.

Doja was furious, he hated being qualified with such a word, but he controlled his nerves. Seeing that he was out of control, Adigun ran to the backyard to fetch another harmful object. Doja hurried towards Amope, to see how she was faring. Debisi felt relaxed a little at her brother's emergence. Amope said she was okay, but rather begged him to check on Okiki. Doja rushed to see his little brother who was just coming back to consciousness.

Suddenly Doja felt a hot stick coming towards his neck. Debisi and Amope had seen Adigun reappear in the hut with firewood that still had a glowing ember. They screamed, and Doja flinched sideways. Adigun missed and lost a little balance. Furiously he jumped towards his son, and Doja swung the pestle in his hand defensively. The pestle caught Adigun at the back of his head, and he fell down drowsily. Adigun lay still.

"My husband, my husband," Amope shouted. She tried crawling towards him, but Debisi held her back.

"Is he dead?" Amope asked, terrified.

Doja just shook his head and looked away from his mother. The atrocious act in the hut had died down. Okiki, who was just regaining his strength, could see his brother limping towards him. The firewood Adigun was holding had struck and seared Doja's thigh, when Adigun charged at him the second time. But he endured the pain. Doja sat beside Okiki, and laid his little brother's hands in his'. The hut was quiet, except for their heavy heartbeats. They did not talk to one another.

Then they heard a sudden ruffle. Before they could tell what it was, Adigun sprang up, picked his bag, and dashed out of the hut.

— 7 —

If the truth were
to be told

S HE WAITED IN the forlorn hope that he would come
back home. But he did not come. Amope began to
emaciate under the weight of her husband's departure.
She lamented. Her children's pleas could not alleviate her
sorrow.

The home was now rid of trouble. But it seemed
another storm was lurking around the corner for Amope's
family. The sudden departure of Adigun and the incidents
that caused it had stirred a wild rumour around the village.
Doja's name was now on the lips of everyone in the village.

The rumour had it that Doja had attempted to kill his father with a pestle. And Adigun had fled from the village for his dear life. The eavesdroppers had corroborated the story with the several altercations that had ensued between Doja and his father, which pointed to the fact that the former would one day kill his father. Amope's name was not mentioned. The rumour-mongers were fair enough not to accuse her of any vice towards her husband. But they suspected Doja was a bastard!

Doja had also heard the rumour. And his world became encapsulated in morose. He averted his eyes whenever he came across any villager. He did not talk to anyone. He became sadder as each day passed. He began to stay away from his family. He knew his kind intervention to salvage his mother's life had been misconceived by the villagers. Amope had not said a word about the matter, and he felt she also accused him. Day after day, Doja drew further into his shell, and he needed just a consolation from the only person who understood him.

Okiki had also been caught in the whole mishap. He had heard the rumours too. And mostly, he worried about his mother's health. He needed consolation too, and he knew just where to get it. He paid the cashew tree an urgent visit.

"Life has two seasons." The cashew tree spoke.

"Tell me." Okiki was eager to know. His mind was disturbed, and he needed urgent answers.

"Life has its good and bad season." The cashew tree answered.

"Life is unfair!" Okiki exclaimed.

He wondered why life ought to be like that. The cashew tree did not respond. The atmosphere was serene. Okiki slipped downwards to his knees, and began sobbing. The little boy was deeply hurt by the way life's deeds had blown his way. The last time he had wished his father was not with them. And now that he got the freedom he wanted, still life had been unfair to him and his siblings. He could foresee trouble following his elder brother's withdrawal from everyone. He needed answers. He cried for a change.

The wind began to blow at him with an unimaginable crescendo. Every packet of breeze was thrown at him. He breathed in dusts. And he coughed out. The wind subsided and everything became calm again.

"You don't have to complain about what happens to you. Rather, you should think of a way out, because the answers to our problems are always around us." The cashew tree spoke calmly.

Okiki wiped his tears. And he looked up at the tree. The boy knew he needed to listen. So he calmed down, and lent his ears to the words of wisdom.

"Life is not unfair," the cashew tree began, "why don't you wait for the good season, and you will see how beautiful life could be. Life can be seen as a farm, and the deeds of men are like seeds. What you are experiencing today is a harvest of what had been sown in the past. Start preparing for the future you wish to experience."

Okiki wished everyone in his house could hear the cashew tree speaking. He wished all the villagers could hear the cashew tree. He wished for more. The cashew tree was pleased Okiki was elated. And he encouraged the little boy to return home. Okiki got up, and left in gratitude.

"Do not forget, life can be seen like a farm, and don't forget it will take some time before you reap all you have sown."

Okiki could hear the cashew tree, as he left. He now understood better. And he understood patience was the key to unlocking a bright future. The cashew tree had not told him a way out of his present predicament, but he knew if he looked inward, the answer would be there.

Kasali had been the first person to visit Amope after the disappearance of her husband. Amope knew Adigun hardly did anything without telling his friend, but Kasali denied knowing Adigun's whereabouts. Amope cried and begged him, but he insisted on having no knowledge of his friend's whereabouts. Debisi, who was at home with Amope when Kasali visited, knew there was lie on Kasali's lips. Debisi often saw Kasali as a mischievous man, and knew at these trying times, his words could not be trusted. Amope also knew Kasali's words could not be counted on, because he and her husband were like the proverbial birds of a feather that would surely flock together.

Doja's succour did come early enough. Jomi sent him a heartfelt message. He sat on the tuft grass on the hill where they had always met, and read the long letter. Jomi's message was gripping and concise. Just as weeds grow apace, the disturbing news had reached her in the city. She wrote to her lover how badly she knew he must have been feeling, and she wished she was there for him. She suggested that he ignored whatever the rumour-mongers were saying, since she trusted him and knew he could not do such a thing.

"*At this point, I suggest you come over to the city. Together we can search for your father.*" Doja read the last line of the letter over and over again. His mind lingered over the choice. He knew the city was too big a place to look for a single man. And he equally understood the culture of the city was such that every man cared for himself, as such, searching for his father was like looking for a pin in a haystack. Moreover, he just couldn't leave his mother alone during these sad moments. And even if he chose to travel to the city in search of his father, the villagers would have alleged him of fleeing the village out of guilt. Doja was the spearhead of the family, and he would have to confront the challenges ahead. He declined Jomi's offer. He stayed.

Okiki's voice was feeble and dry, but had the tenderness that could touch Amope's heart. Mother and son were alone in the hut. Debisi had gone to the market, and Doja was away as usual. And Okiki knew this was his opportunity to talk to his mother alone. Doja had declined from talking to her, since he felt she also agreed he was the cause of his father's disappearance. But Debisi had tried severally, and failed.

"Mother can't you see our home is falling apart?" Okiki challenged. The little boy's words hit Amope. She looked up at her last child. But the little boy continued.

"Mother we need you now more than ever. Please pull yourself together." Okiki begged.

The little boy's voice sang a symphony in the bereaved mother's heart. Her eyes lifted up. And she broke into a benign smile. She could not believe her little boy could be the one now encouraging her. She could see strength and leadership in the innocent boy's eyes. His few words had encouraged her greatly. And she realised there was still much to receive, than what she thought she had lost.

"I believe father would still come back home," Okiki added.

"I believe too." Amope replied faintly.

Okiki smiled, and ran into his mother's waiting arms. Amope held her little son in a hearty embrace, and quietly thanked God for blessing her with such a dear child.

"We will not let you down, mother. We will take good care of you." Okiki assured.

"Yes you all will." Amope retorted gladly.

Amope's disposition towards her children changed from that day. It seemed an elixir had swung her back into youthfulness. Debisi wondered what magic or therapy had worked on her. But they were all glad to come together as a small happy family. Amope had called Doja privately, and had a long persuasive talk with him. And Doja now understood he misconstrued his mother's reactions towards him.

Okiki was glad the idea had worked. He had used his inner strength just as his mysterious friend had taught, but had also followed the advice of his schoolteacher; Mary.

Mary had noticed that a mood of melancholy descended on Okiki. At first she ignored, but when she saw the mood was lasting for too long and was having adverse effects on Okiki's learning. She called him for a private talk. Okiki refused to say a word. He saw Mary as a stranger, and he felt it was improper for him to discuss his family issues with her. Mary let him be. And Okiki avoided her eyes during class. Mary never took offence in his improper conduct. She knew he was just being childish. Moreover, she often saw her late brother in Okiki's eyes, and she naturally had a soft spot for him.

Another opportunity came, when Jomi sent her second letter. Mary had asked Okiki to come for the letter when the school was over that day. Okiki had collected the letter and wanted to leave, when she called him back.

"I seem to take so much interest in you because I once had a brother of your age who died years back." Okiki was rooted to the spot by Mary's words. He suddenly felt so much sympathy for his class-teacher, and he waited.

"Am so sorry to hear about his loss," Okiki replied.

"Thanks. But am sure you don't know a problem shared is half-solved?" Mary retorted. Seeing that he was listening, she waved him to sit next to her, and told him to shed the weight on his mind.

Mary's soulfulness was radiant in her eyes, as she listened to Okiki's sad story. She felt so much pity for the poor boy, as he narrated his mother's ordeal and his father's sudden disappearance. Okiki sobbed as he spoke. Mary knew she had to proffer a quick solution to the little boy's domestic problem, since the promotional examination was fast approaching. At first she offered to pay Okiki's mother a kind visit, but Okiki said her mother would feel uncomfortable by such visit. And so, she advised him to summon some courage and talk to his mother, since he was her favourite.

Okiki was eager to see his class-teacher, after school period that Monday. Her suggestion had worked, and he had many reasons to thank her. Mary could also see the brightness in his eyes too, and was sure the idea had worked. Truly, when the chance came, Okiki thanked her profusely, and Mary was happy her labour of love had eventually paid off. Okiki was about to leave, but Mary told him to wait a little because she wanted to tell him a story. Okiki sat and listened with rapt attention.

"There was once a boy who passed through great difficulties at childhood. He had been born to his mother during trying times, because she had been barren for many years and her husband's first wife already had many children, before God eventually blessed her with him. She loved him dearly, and her husband loved him more and even sowed the little boy a special robe of many colours. The little boy turned out to be a child of promise because he once dreamt his brothers, and his parents would someday bow before him. His father cherished

the dream but the boy's brothers hated him. They hated him so much that they planned to kill him but eventually sold him into slavery, and lied to their father that he had been killed by a wild animal. The helpless boy passed through great difficulties as a slave, and was later sent to prison for a crime he did not commit."

"Okiki would you believe me if I told you that this boy eventually became a leader in a foreign land?" Mary asked.

"You don't mean it?" Okiki asked in total surprise.

"Yes, he became the second most important person in a land where he was once a slave and a prisoner. And his brothers and parents came and bowed before him." Mary replied. Okiki was totally confounded by the story, and wished he was the boy.

"The boy's name is Joseph. And someday, you could be as great as him." Mary concluded.

Okiki was awestruck by his class-teacher's conclusion. He never knew he shared a name with someone of great importance. Before he could ask why she told him the story, Mary said she had noticed his discomfiture since the day she called him 'Joseph the Dreamer' and knew she had to tell him the whole truth about the boy called Joseph.

That day, Okiki sauntered all the way back to the village, as if he had all the time in the world. He felt like a king. And knew someday, he could be. He felt greatly relieved knowing the story of Joseph, and why he was called a dreamer. And he believed if Joseph could overcome all odds, he certainly could too. But mostly, he remembered the exact words his dear class-teacher had used to summarize it all up *"tough times never last, but tough people do."* He knew his family would be glad to hear the story, especially his mother. He walked home happily.

— 8 —

Renegade!

A CCUSATIONS AND CONTRADICTIONS were far from being swept under the grass for Doja. It had been seven months since Adigun disappeared from the village. And the news of how he disappeared was still wagging on the tongues of the villagers. Doja turned deaf ears to their words, but there was certain emptiness in his bowels; a void in his mind. A feeling that made him felt guilty, after all. He knew unless his father came back home, the whole truth about his intent would not come to limelight.

Jomi had sent him another urgent letter. She wanted him to strike the iron while it was still hot. She told him to avail himself the opportunity of following the lorry that conveyed people from the village to the city every Fridays. She promised to be waiting for him every Friday evening at the park, until he eventually showed up.

The virtuous young lady wanted her lover to show some sincere concern about the sudden departure of his father. But Doja felt there was no reason for such. He knew his father had left with his concubine, even if the whole village didn't care to know. His father's departure was good riddance to bad rubbish. Doja just couldn't bear coming face-to-face with his father again. Anger brewed in his mind, as he tore the letter.

Amope also felt a vacuum in her heart, but the progress of her little boy seemed to fill the vacuum. Okiki had promoted to the next class, and she was proud her son was soaring in the western knowledge. The little boy's future gave her a lot of hope. And she certainly knew someday, Okiki would definitely wipe away her tears.

Okiki was also glad that he was performing brilliantly at school. His classmates now envied him because he was topping the class in all subjects. They believed his intimacy with their class-teacher gave him a favourable advantage over them. But little did they know that Okiki burned the midnight candles, and ensured his mind was open to learning.

The friendship between Mary and Okiki had truly moistened. The two became fond of each other. At first, Okiki declined from receiving snacks from his teacher, but later consented, since he never wanted to offend her in any way. He really enjoyed eating the snacks. Unlike the bean-cake he was familiar with in the village, Mary brought him meat-pies and doughnuts, which were definitely foreign snacks. Okiki got to know Mary better and realised her parents were both educated and living in the city. In fact, her father was a Principal of a secondary school in the city. Mary had come to work in the village in order to hone her teaching skills before travelling to Europe for her university education. Mary assured Okiki that would be many years to come, and the little boy's fears were alleviated.

After school each day, Mary accompanied Okiki to the market square, before returning back to her home. Okiki became fond of her, just as she was too. On a certain day, Mary decided to take Okiki to the hill. Okiki was dumbfounded when he saw that the bushy path had unfurled in the end, opening a vast space of imagination before him.

"This is where I and Jomi always came to spend our leisure time."

Okiki had heard Mary. He had understood they were intimate friends, and they shared a lot in common. But his eyes wandered from the acacia tree whose branches spanned over the quiet hill, to the tuft grasses that carpeted the surface of the hill. Most of all, he could see the pure stream, sailing gently, far beneath the hill. It was such a beautiful sight. But Okiki also feared staring downwards into the stream, with the feeling that he may fall of the hill. Mary sat safely under the tree, and Okiki quickly sat down beside her.

Okiki watched as Mary threw a pebble down into the stream. He was excited by the way the pebble caused ripples on the water. He loved as the ripples moved from close circles into wide circles, until they vanished, and the course of the gentle stream continued. Mary could see the ripples had caught his attention, and she threw another pebble. She encouraged Okiki to do likewise, and the two of them smiled at the ripples, in the cool afternoon, under the shade of the acacia tree.

"Okiki, what can you see?" Mary asked.

"I can see ripples." He replied.

"What came to your mind when you saw the ripples?" She asked further.

"Nothing," he replied, wondering what she was driving at. He listened quietly, as she spoke.

"Firstly, we can assume that the life of a man is like the course of the gentle stream, and the ripples are like adversities of life. Since you noticed that the ripples appeared for a while and later disappeared, this means that there would certainly be tough times, but the truth is that they will only be for a while. The adversities would surely disappear someday." Mary explained.

He had often seen ripples on the stream at the village river, but he had never felt there could be such a rare wisdom in one of the evidences of nature. He smiled, as Mary continued.

"We can also liken the stream to be the length of a human life, and the ripples as the impact people make in their lifetime. You saw how a tiny impact on the stream caused the ripples, and you also saw how the ripples expanded across the surface of the stream, that's just the way your little effort can make a lot of changes too. It is the effect of ripples you make during your lifetime that people would talk about after you are gone." Mary concluded.

After Okiki left Mary that day and went home, the introspection about the ripples held sway on his mind. He thought deeply about it. He realised what she taught him was also similar to the life lessons he received from the mysterious tree. He now believed the adversities would not last. And he also understood he could paint a great picture with his life. The lonely child braced up for the challenges ahead.

The smell of fallen rain transcend across Irewolu village that Saturday afternoon. A heavy rain had just fallen, and the whole sky was blanketed with whiteness. The grasses lit with such freshness, as the spirits of the little village children seemed to be ignited by the rain. Amope and her children were inside the hut about to have their lunch. They had hardly settled down to eat when they heard a certain noise outside. Amope jumped up, and they all hurried behind her.

Two women scurried towards their hut. Suddenly, as they neared the hut, they slammed themselves on the muddy floor, and threw their shawls in the air. Amope and her children were confused, as they ran to help the two women.

"Why has this happened to us?" The two women lamented, as they rolled themselves in the mud.

"What is going on?" Amope queried.

"It's your husband, it's your husband." The women chorused, as they refused to be calmed down.

Debisi stayed closely behind her mother, while Doja held Okiki's hand warmly. Amope felt fooled by the situation around her, as she could not grasp what was going on. But certainly with the way the two women were reacting, she knew definitely something had gone wrong somewhere. Something bad had happened. And it had a lot to do with her husband, as the women had mentioned. Three village elders now approached the hut. Amope hurried to meet them,

"Please, what is going on?" Amope queried.

"Calm down, Amope." The elders replied, and called Doja aside. When they had moved beyond earshot, the men surrounded Doja and told him how the rope at the well was broken, and the water jar got shattered. Doja felt a sudden pang in his heart. He held to himself tightly, as the men told him to show much fortitude and comfort his mother and siblings.

Amope was obviously worried and tensed. She wondered why her first child would be called apart. Doja and the elders were now moving back towards Amope and the others, when a loud wailing noise descended around their hut. A wooden coffin was laid on the shoulders of two hefty men approaching the hut, and the villagers surrounding the coffin wore a troubled look, while the women with them wailed.

"What is it? What is it?" Amope became most nervous, as the elderly men and Doja hurried to her side, to hold her.

"It is the city. The city has treated us badly." The wailing woman chorused.

Amope suddenly flung herself to the ground, and burst into loud cries. She had understood where the arrows of pain had hit her. She ululated and refused to be held or comforted. There were now discordant notes of cries, as Adigun's corpse was laid down. Debisi wailed loudly, and could not even come to the aid of her mother who was now being held back by the sympathizers from tearing her clothes. Okiki buried his head inside Doja's chest and cried.

"How did it happen?" The sympathisers asked one another.

"He was crushed by a reckless driver." Someone answered, and there was another high pitch of cries, in front of Adigun's hut.

That night, Amope cursed herself, and her children begged her not to. It was the longest night Okiki ever experienced. No one could sleep. Some kind villagers stayed with them throughout that night; still, there was so much loneliness within the hut. Amope laid her weary head on the shoulders of her daughter, Debisi, and talked to herself inconsistently. Everyone remained silent and allowed their thoughts to feed on them.

Still that night, Okiki hallucinated. Doja had held him in a warm embrace as they sat at a dark corner within the hut. Okiki saw his father's spirit appear at the entrance of the hut. Adigun was covered in a white robe, his face was bruised, and he wore a grey look.

"Why have you done this to us, father?" Okiki demanded.

The innocent boy had a lot on his mind. He felt disappointed by his father's sudden demise. He had hoped his father would someday return to them. And he knew how pleased their mother would be. While he lived, he had brought their mother so much pain, and now that he was dead, he had brought her much more pain. And this was such a big stigma that would go down into the rumours of their village.

Suddenly, Okiki could see his father's ghost turn its back towards him, and walked away. The question he asked had caused a sudden guilt within his father. As the ghost disappeared into the night, a reply was given. Okiki heard just a word. It was clear, loud and distinct.

"Nemesis"

Okiki stirred up in riposte, as Doja shrugged him out of his hallucination. The innocent boy looked around and outside the hut, and saw no ghost. The atmosphere in the hut was still melancholic. He rubbed his eyes, leaned back on his elder brother, and kept this secret to himself.

Some of the village elders accompanied Doja to his father's grave, the following morning. Amope and the other children had been asked to stay back at home. Doja watched as his father was laid into the ground, and he was asked to perform the burial rites of dust-to-dust. That morning, Doja cried. He had felt a sudden turmoil on his mind, even if he had disliked his father; death certainly wasn't a way of settling their quarrel.

Kasali and his wife, Asake, were not far from Amope's hut. They had also spent the first long night with them, even though Amope did not take notice of them, because there were quite a sizeable number of sympathisers in the small hut, on the day Adigun's corpse was brought home. But they had remained frequent, in the subsequent days. The number of sympathisers reduced, as Amope began her traditional forty days of mourning her husband. But Kasali and his wife, paid a constant visit to the house, and their presence was much appreciated.

Kasali was deeply hurt by his friend's demise. He knew how much he tried to dissuade his friend from running to the city with his concubine. The secret was heavy in his heart because everyone still believed Adigun had fled from his home because his son had revolted against him. Kasali's conscience pricked him, and he felt the only way to assuage such guilty conscience was to support Amope and her children in the best way he could. Asake and Amope weren't intimate friends, because the latter was older that the former. Asake was such a jealous woman, and she had followed her husband daily since she once caught his eyes preying on Amope's nubile daughter, Debisi.

Doja was returning from the farm one day when he caught two young boys fighting one another. He tried to stop the duel, but the stronger boy insisted on beating up the weaker one. Doja shouted at the recalcitrant boy, and threatened to wallop him. But was shocked by the boy's response,

"Are you going to kill me just like you killed your father?"

The words rattled in Doja's head. He was rooted to the spot as the two boys left. The fresh rumour was already on the lips of all the villagers. Everywhere he passed, he could overhear them calling him a murderer. Okiki and Debisi had not heard. And Amope was still mourning indoors, so she did not hear too.

The weight was becoming too much for Doja to bear. His mind ruminated for long, empty hours. And he kept to himself. He wished he had gone to the city in search for his father, just as Jomi had suggested. If he had, probably he would have found his father and brought him back home, or otherwise, if Adigun had eventually died, he would be too far away to feel the sting of the villagers. He now blamed himself more. But a twisty decision dangled between his chest, and he lingered over the choice, as he returned back to the village that day.

"Impetuous child," a voice bellowed, as Doja passed by the cashew tree.

Doja heard the voice. He waited and looked around, but saw no one. He felt probably he had thought aloud. The cashew tree knew Doja's next intention, and had wanted to dissuade him from taking such rash steps. The cashew tree pitied Doja because his intentions towards his family were good, but he never clearly thought them out before he took action.

"Your impetuosity is only exceeded by your impetuosity." The cashew tree bellowed again.

But this time, Doja did not hear. The bereaved young man walked home with so much feeling of heaviness. That night Doja had a terrible nightmare. In his dream, the villagers had ganged up to stone him to death. Beads of sweat broke across his forehead, as he woke up that midnight. He knew he had to take a quick step before such a terrible dream turned to reality.

But earlier that afternoon, while Doja was away, Debisi was surprised to see a stranger in front of their hut. The stranger was a slim, fair-skinned, young lady. Debisi knew she was slightly older than her, and the stranger's presence wore such a remarkable dignity. And she kind of liked her at once.

"Please, is this where Okiki lives?" Mary enquired.

"Yes," Debisi replied, and led her into the hut.

Okiki's jaws dropped as Mary entered into the hut. He had been absent from school for over two weeks, and Mary had become worried about the absence of one of her students. The school regulations had required she sought the welfare of her students, in case one of them was absent for lengthy days. But her heart had also wanted to see her little friend. She felt so much loneliness in her heart, everyday she looked at Okiki's chair, and saw it was still vacant. She feared nothing bad had happened to him. Every night, she silently prayed for him.

Amope and Debisi watched as Okiki sprang up, and ran into the waiting arms of the strange lady.

"Mother, this is my class-teacher." Okiki introduced.

Amope was equally delighted to see Mary. Okiki had told her a lot of wonderful things about Mary, and she was pleased to have her kind presence in their hut. Mary greeted Okiki's mother, and teased her for giving birth to such a wonderful boy. Mary refused to be entertained, since she had actually come to check on the welfare of her student. But she was deeply surprised to find Okiki hale and hearty, except that the mood in the hut was in low spirits.

Okiki led her out, and told her why he had been absent from school. Mary shuddered all over. A marshmallow of sensations swept over her. She could not believe her ears. She tried so much to hold back the tears, as that might trigger fresh tears within the hut. Mary felt so much pity for the poor boy and his helpless mother. She totally accepted Okiki's decision to stay with his mother during the mourning-period, and she promised to take him through the missed lessons when he resumed back in school. Mary returned back into the hut, stooped before Amope, and comforted her for a while before she departed.

Mary's visitation to their hut that day brought so much relief to the little home, because for the first time in over two weeks of mourning they had something fresh and bright to talk and think about. Doja was the only one that did not feel the breeze, because he was not at home when Mary visited.

Probably if Doja had met Mary, he would have had a second thought. Amope's forty days of mourning brought Doja so much torture. He had sleepless nights. And he had no one to talk to. But he patiently stood by his mother during the mourning-period, as it was the last respect he owed her. Before anyone woke up in the hut, on the following day that ended Amope's mourning, Doja sneaked out of the hut at dawn on a Friday, and joined the lorry to the city.

— 9 —

Sometimes our hands are tied

THAT NIGHT, AMOPE cried. She had been forced to make a decision she didn't want to. But she had been pushed to a corner, and left with no other option. Debisi cried too, because her life had been caught in the line. And she would have to lay her life down as a price for her mothers'.

It all began on the day Doja ran to the city. Amope had first disregarded it as cheap rumour. Doja's clothes and things had remained in the hut. And she believed there was no reason for her first son to desert her. But when that day passed, and the second day passed too. It finally dawned on her that she had just two children left to herself.

Amope was in total turmoil. She wondered where she had gone wrong. Doja did not leave any message. Neither did she take notice of his stranger behaviours before he left. Her eyes were too crumpled in tears, to notice Doja's disposition towards everyone. Her heart was too saddened by the sudden loss of her husband to have time to understand what was going on in the minds of any of her children.

It was Debisi who solved the riddle. She figured out that her brother had fled to the city, because some of the villagers had labelled him a murderer. Amope was displeased by the news.

"People of Irewolu, if you can't alleviate my suffering, you shouldn't add to it." Amope cried.

The helpless widow found companion in solitude. She loved Doja so much; he was her first child, and his presence in her life could not be rivalled. She wished her son had talked to her about it. She wished she could bring him back home. Her heart was heavy. She was losing taste for food. And her health was deteriorating. Okiki and Debisi begged her to come to terms with the situation and move on. But they all landed on deaf ears.

Okiki equally did not relent in searching for his brother. He ran to Mary for assistance. Mary was disappointed by the news too. She knew Doja must definitely have run to Jomi in the city. And she felt Jomi had not made a wise decision by allowing Doja to stay with her. But she wasn't in a hurry to judge her friend either. After all, love had its own way of complicating things. And so she felt it would not be wise to write Jomi about it.

Okiki had wanted Mary to write a letter to Jomi in the city, asking Doja to return to the village because his mother's health was deteriorating. But Mary persuaded Okiki to leave his brother alone. And also desist from searching for him. She knew they had to be extremely cautious about the matter. She understood Doja was a full grown man. He must have thought deeply before taking such a rash decision. Writing Jomi about the whole matter might shatter their relationship, and Doja might even leave Jomi, and flee to a place where no one could reach or contact him. And that would be worse.

"Some things are not meant to be hurried. Calm down Okiki. We must wait for the right time." Mary begged.

Okiki left Mary displeased. But he did not show it. He ran to meet the mysterious old tree for assistance.

"Is it true that my brother is with his fiancée, Jomi, in the city?" Okiki queried, pacing up and down.

The cashew tree was surprised by the way Okiki spoke. The young boy had mistaken the mysterious tree for a spiritual medium. The cashew tree went into a boisterous roar of laughter. The wind blew in quick rasps. The cashew tree's leaves and branches shook violently, and a cashew fruit dropped on Okiki's head. The young boy gave a short cry, and held his head.

"What if I had said I didn't have any idea about your brother's whereabouts?" The tree retorted.

Okiki now calmed down. He realised he was abusing the relationship between him and the mysterious tree. He patiently narrated what had happened in the past few weeks, and sought for the cashew tree's advice. The cashew tree listened carefully.

"I suggest you heed to Mary's advice." The tree advised.

"But I think she is not trying to help me out." Okiki retorted.

"It may seem so, but she is right. Your brother's impetuosity had led him into all this trouble. And until he learns his lessons, every attempt to bring him home would escalate into more trouble."

"What about my mother's health?" Okiki begged.

"Go home and help your mother. And beware of the wolf in sheep's skin."

The cashew tree ended the discussion, and Okiki left. The young boy was growing into a man, and he was now having more responsibilities on his shoulders. The biggest responsibility for him was keeping a secret from his mother. He knew where his elder brother was, but he had to keep mute. Okiki wondered what the mysterious tree meant by 'a wolf in sheep's skin'. He also had a lot on his mind to think about, and he didn't want to bother himself with such matters. He returned home.

Jomi's eyes gleamed with so much amusement on the first day Doja arrived in the city. She was excited to see the love of her life again. Even though his dressing that day was totally awkward for city life, still she felt so proud of him. Doja was equally excited to see her. Her beauty glittered under the afternoon sun. And he could hardly take his eyes off her. But he did not show it. Neither did he say a word. His mind was heavy with the incidents that preceded his coming to the city.

Three days passed before the love birds eventually had time to talk. Jomi wanted Doja to have some time to rest. And also acclimatize with the city life. Doja did rest. His mind marvelled at all the civilised things in Jomi's house. Jomi had fondly teased they were electric objects, whenever Doja enquired about an object or two. And he also understood that the objects could electrify him to death if he was not careful. And so whenever Jomi was at work, he was careful enough not to touch the electric objects. And he preferred looking at the beautiful world outside through the windows. The city was totally different, from the village. It was a civilised world, and Doja wondered if he would ever return to the village. He seemed pleased with the city.

"So when do you want us to start searching for your father?" Jomi asked.

Since Doja arrived, he had not said a thing about the village. Jomi observed he was quite moody, but she felt it was all about his missing father.

"Father is dead." Doja replied coldly.

Jomi was shocked by the news. She was more surprised by the way Doja had said it. She saw that his look was cold, and discouraging. She wondered why he had not said anything about it, since he arrived from the village. She now wondered why Doja came to the city since his father was dead. She held her peace, and did not say a word.

"I want to stay in the city." Doja remarked.

Jomi did not believe her ears. The two lovers stared at each other for a long time. Doja was thinking Jomi would reject him, since he had not informed her earlier. And the manner in which he had come to the city ought to be questioned. But instead, Jomi was really excited by the news. She was glad to have her fiancé next to her. She hurried towards him and hugged him. Doja held her tightly, and heaved a sigh of great relief.

Debisi and Okiki could not heave a sigh of relief. Instead, they ran around the hut trying to save Amope's life. Fortunately or unfortunately, Kasali materialised in the hut that moment. Since Adigun died, and Doja fled to the city, Kasali had shown immense support for the poor widow. Debisi knew he could not be trusted, but the current situation around them made her ignore such thoughts. Kasali's presence in their lives was greatly felt, and Amope found no reason to think otherwise.

Amope was thrown into another epilepsy fit. Debisi and Okiki cried as they could not help their mother. Amope went through violent and horrible movements on the hard floor. She foamed at the mouth, and it seemed she was taking her final breath. Kasali did not show any form of awe as Amope went through the frightful mess. Although his late friend had told him his wife was an epileptic, but the scene did not seem to irritate Kasali a bit.

"I can help you out."

That was what Kasali said, after the fit subsided. Amope was not sure she had heard him right. She wondered what manner of man he was. He had watched her go through such agony. And he was now willing to proffer a solution. Debisi and Okiki turned their heads fully to hear what Kasali had to say.

"I know a native doctor that can cure your sickness." Kasali noted.

The sound of a native doctor made Amope feel slightly uncomfortable. She was not willing to trust her life with one. She knew most of them to be quacks and liars. But her sickness was getting beyond control. It was bringing her much embarrassment, and if she did not find a solution to it soon, it may eventually take her life. She agreed to go with Kasali.

Okiki had a lot on his mind too. Since Doja had left, Okiki also had to start spending some quality hours each day on the farm with his sister. He had missed school for quite some weeks. And so he also had to spend many hours writing the class notes. And also spend extra hours studying them. Mary was fully supportive, and she ensured the pressure was not too much for the young boy. Okiki was very optimistic and excited by Kasali's offer. "If that was the way out, his mother had better taken it," he thought to himself, since he was getting scared of his mother's dear life.

The path to the native doctor's abode was such a lengthy one. Kasali, Amope and Debisi had to brush the tall, huge elephant grasses cropping across the path with the back of their hands. Debisi's mind doubted as they went: it was such a deserted road. She wondered who must have brought Kasali, and what must have led him to such a secluded area. Amope did not think in such manner. The poor woman believed nothing good would come easy. "If this was the way out of her predicament, she would rather stick her neck to it," She thought. Okiki was not taken along.

The first thing the native doctor, a short man with rough whiskers told Amope was that the sickness had been inflicted on her by someone very close to her. Amope was less surprised, because she truly wasn't born with the sickness. It started a few months after the birth of Okiki. The thought of someone close to her inflicting her with such illness left her wondering who the person could be, and where she had gone wrong to deserve such.

Debisi's eyes wandered from one fetish object to another. She listened as the native doctor chanted panegyrics. The small hut with a thatch roof had a grim and dreary look. A strong unpleasant smell hung in the air. Debisi noticed Kasali's eyes were on her as they listened to the native doctor. She felt uncomfortable.

"So, what is the cure?" Kasali cuts in.

The native doctor did not waste time in listing all the ingredients needed to cure Amope of her epilepsy sickness. The ingredients were scarce to find, and it required a huge sum of money to buy them. Amope had nowhere to get the money. But she became more perplexed when the native doctor told them that if a remedy was not given urgently, the sickness might cost her life.

"I will bring the money." Kasali replied.

Amope was surprised. Debisi could not believe her ears either. The native doctor turned to him, and asked if he was Amope's husband, and he replied in the negative. Kasali explained Amope's plight to the native doctor, and said he was doing her this favour on behalf of his intimate friend. The native doctor reasoned with him, and equally thanked him for his extreme generosity. Amope's lips were filled with gratitude for Kasali.

"I have a strange feeling about all this." Debisi remarked when they got back home.

Okiki was the only person she told this. And Amope was far from sight when she told him. The young boy wondered why his elder sister made such conclusion, after explaining Kasali's generosity towards salvaging their mother's life. He did not show any form of disapproval to what his sister said. Neither did he show any form of acceptance. He kept quiet and did not say a word. But he kept her words in his heart.

Amope returned back to high-spiritedness and vivacity. That was a few weeks after she went through the rigorous fetish deliverance. The native doctor's cure had worked, and they were all certain about it. But they waited several months after just to be sure Amope was totally fit. She often had her epilepsy crisis once in four months. But many months passed, and Okiki promoted to another class, and still Amope showed no sign of illness. Her children were excited to see her in full bloom again. Okiki wished Doja was around to witness it all.

Amope felt indebted to Kasali, not knowing how to repay him. She knew deep down her mind that such a favour needed to be repaid, but she did not know which way it would be done. Kasali had been frequent in their house. And made sure Amope's health was upbeat. Asake was already tired of following her husband around, since he left no clues. And most times, he never told his wife whenever he was going to pay the widow a visit. Asake was left in the dark; she had no idea about what transpired between Kasali and Amope.

"I want to have your daughter's hands in marriage." Kasali voiced out, during one of his usual visits.

Kasali was certain his request could not be rejected. Amope was speechless. Kasali's financial succour to save her life was worth more than Debisi's bride price. Kasali had proved to the widow that he could be trusted and leaned on. But Amope wondered how her daughter would feel if she begged her to sacrifice her marital dreams as a way of repaying Kasali for his kindness. She equally wondered how Kasali's wife, Asake, would feel if she learns that Debisi would become her rival in Kasali's house.

And so, that night, Amope cried. She had been forced to make a decision she didn't want to. She had been pushed to a corner, and left with no other option. Debisi cried too, because her life had been caught in the line. But her mother's joy was uttermost on her mind. Debisi agreed to lay her life down as a price for her mothers'. Kasali paid no bride price.

——10——

Mother and Son

DOJA SANK HEAVILY into the sofa. He had just returned back from work. He hated the bank security job. The uniform; the beret; even the big black boots gave him blisters during the first few months he began the job. At first, his duty was to monitor the banking hall; he enjoyed the freshness of the air condition, and the tips he got from kind customers. But lately, he had been transferred to the bank gate, and the act of opening and shutting the wide gate made him weary. He also took record of every car that came in and left the bank. Worst of all, the bank customers did not even take notice of his exhausting job; he got no tip.

Doja earned a liveable salary, and he was not pleased with it. At first, he was pleased with the take home package, but later he realised he was not qualified for some financial benefits in his workplace, and he resented such. He also realised other staff were being promoted based on their qualification, and he was not, because he had no educational qualification. He detested such.

He understood his duty in the bank to be the laborious type, and also brain-tasking. As such, he wondered why the educated bankers in their gay tradition, with the comfortable duty of counting money, and imputing figures had to earn more than him. He got to his place of work early, and left late. He felt this was pure discrimination, and his once lovable job now seemed to bore him. It was now ten months since he fled from the village.

"How was work today?" Jomi asked, as she emerged from the kitchen.

Doja did not respond. He was not ready to be repeating words like a broken gramophone. He had complained several times to Jomi about his job, and her usual response on being patient or contented made him sick to the stomach. He now seemed to envy her because she earned a decent living as a clerk in an accounting firm. And her so called 'comfortable' salary; which was thrice his' made him feel inadequate as her husband. He snickered off his whiskers.

Jomi chose to keep silent rather than ask him what he was sniggering at. She also ignored his rude approach at not responding to her question. She sat opposite him, and looked at him with much displeasure. She got him the job. And she knew she had been very lucky to help him secure such a dignifying job, despite his non-qualification. She realised Doja was now taking her for granted. And he did not seem to recognise or appreciate her efforts at securing him the job.

As a young woman, she worried more about when Doja would take her back to the village for a proper traditional marriage. She knew he now had more than enough money in his savings to pay for her bride price. And they living together as a couple in the city without a proper marriage ceremony made Jomi feel uncomfortable. She realised Doja resented the whole idea the first time she raised it. She almost got slapped the second time she brought up the issue. And she now seemed to wonder if this was the man she once knew. She worried if she had not started her life on the wrong footing.

But Debisi didn't have to doubt where her life was heading towards. She knew she had started her own life on the wrong step. And she would have to face the odds and take her chances too. Her arrival in Kasali's house was met with a strong resistance. Asake, Kasali's first wife showed a strong dislike for her, and it made home very uncomfortable for Debisi. Kasali did not care about her welfare; rather he treated her like a maid servant.

Amope had also felt a tinge of the hostility too. Asake had stormed her hut the second day Debisi moved to Kasali's house. Amope succumbed as Asake yelled at her, and called her unprintable names. Asake's voice was loud enough for all the neighbours and prying animals to hear. Okiki watched as the woman, who was less than her mother's age drubbing his mother on the pitch of shame. He was furious, and his countenance showed it. But Amope did not say a word.

"Please don't kill my husband like you killed yours." Asake hollered as she left their hut.

Mother and son stared at each other blankly. Okiki was pregnant with words. He wanted to ask why his mother had taken such a decision. Rumours had been going around the village that Amope sold her daughter to her husband's best friend because poverty was eating her up. Okiki was sure the rumours must have landed on his mother's ears too. But he sensed a caution, not to accuse or bother his mother about such. He hurried towards her, and hugged her, since he knew having her meant more to him than any other thing. Amope held him in a soulful embrace, and knew her last child would someday heal her wounds and wipe her tears.

Kasali, a true leopard which would not change its spots, showed his true nature once he got what he wanted. He stopped visiting Amope. And he did not care about her welfare anymore. He had heard about the embarrassment Asake had caused Amope, and he did not bother to go back and apologise for his wife's misbehaviour. Instead, he avoided passing in front of her hut. Amope felt like a fool. And the rumour across the village was beginning to eat her up like a canker-worm. The helpless widow wished she could turn back the hands of time.

"Why did mother make such a decision?" Okiki queried.

He was talking to his mysterious friend; the old cashew tree. It was a usual Sunday evening, when most villagers rest in their huts, and the road to the village market was usually deserted. The sun shone brightly high in the sky. But Okiki was safe under the branches of the cashew tree. The two had maintained their secret friendship for four years, and Okiki knew he would forever be grateful to his mysterious friend.

"It is the wise masquerade that takes the last dance at the masquerade festival." The wise old tree replied.

Okiki was confused by the response. He wasn't talking about a masquerade festival, and he wasn't thinking of attending one either.

"What would you have done if you were in her shoes?" The cashew tree asks back.

Seeing that the young boy was silent, and could not give an answer, the cashew tree went on to explain that it was easier to trade faults rather than find solutions. The mysterious tree advised him to look ahead, and also told him to sit patiently and watch as the days go by because time had a way of judging people and their deeds.

Okiki reasoned with the wise tree. But the young boy still had another issue that bothered his heart greatly. Since his elder brother disappeared, he had quite a burden on his neck. But since his sister had been tied in an unwanted marriage too, it seemed as if he carried the burden of the whole world on his shoulders. He worried over how to share his life and time with the schooling hours, farm labour, house chores, and a proper attention for his mother too. He loved his elder sister too, and would want to sneak to her place whenever the opportunity presented itself. He poured out his mind to the old cashew tree, and sought for a way forward.

"There is a way out." The cashew tree retorted after listening to Okiki's lamentation.

"Tell me then." The young boy replied.

Although deep down his mind, Okiki often wished the mysterious could simply wave a magic wand and make all his troubles disappear. Since the tree had the ability of speech and unfathomable wisdom, Okiki guessed it should also be able to work like a spiritual medium. The advice he often got from the cashew tree had always been noble, true and perfect. But the truth was that they were really uncomfortable to practise or comply with. Doing the right thing was difficult and slow. Okiki wished for a short cut that would end all his troubles.

"Go and solve other people's problems, and you will be amazed by the way your problems will be solved too." The cashew tree advised.

Okiki had first wanted to snap back at the cashew tree and say that he knew the mysterious old tree had a way of complicating things and compounding his problems. But he kept mute. And he lent his ears to tutelage.

"Every man must depend on another. You need to reach out to others first. And you will be amazed by the way they will reach out to you too."

"But I don't have what it takes to help others." The confused boy blurted out.

"Yes you do. We have all been created to help one another, and we all have at least one thing our neighbours do not have." The cashew tree expatiated.

Okiki seemed to agree even though he did not really understand the whole idea of helping others. "Would he be going from house to house, asking his neighbours if they needed his help?" He thought to himself.

"No," the cashew tree cuts in, "the opportunity would present itself, and you will have to take your chances." The cashew tree concluded.

Okiki was a bit startled. The cashew tree was able to read his mind. He remembered that was not the first time either. And the young boy realised the mysterious tree must have heard all what he had been thinking about since he arrived there. He felt embarrassed and insecure. And he did not seem to have the boldness to stand at the cashew tree's presence any longer. The young boy ran home.

Mary was quick in coming to Okiki's aid. She understood her little friend to be the type who was often shy to share his problems. She had first seen the brightness in his eyes, during the period his mother's epilepsy got healed. And now she wondered why that brightness had suddenly waned again.

"What's wrong?" Mary asked, during one of their friendly visitations to the hill.

Okiki tugged at the tuft grasses on the hill. He tried to avoid Mary's eyes as he explained how his mother got a cure for her illness, and how his sister's long time happiness was smeared in the process. The words slurred out from his lips. Okiki was not proud of himself. He was getting bored of a relationship which he totally dominated and was quite parasitic. He hardly had good news to share with his doted class-teacher, rather he complained always.

Mary did not feel that way about Okiki. She enjoyed every moment she spent with him, since the years she had known him. He was such a loving little boy. And she had equally promised herself to do for Okiki that which she was unable to do for her late brother. And so she relished every moment she spent with him. Moreover, she admired Okiki for his strength and courage. She wondered how he had been able to pull through such trying times. Even his classmates, who had lesser problems, were tired of school, and some had quit. But as the adversities increased, the young boy's desire to be a better person increased too. His grades in class remained at the top. And his disposition with his colleagues at school was very mutual.

He was now in the penultimate stage of his primary schooling career. And Mary knew she had to stand by him through thick and thin. She wanted to groom him properly for his final year, and especially the scholarship exam which, if he passed, would give him an opportunity to further his secondary school education at the city through full scholarship. Year in year out, none of the pupils of the Missionary primary school had ever scaled the scholarship cut-off mark, because the exam was exceptionally difficult. But with the determination in Okiki's eyes, Mary knew he could scale through. But if he would do so, she needed to give him a lot of academic support, and ensured his mindset was stable. She kept this as a little secret.

"Have you ever considered praying?" Mary suggested.

"Praying," the young boy repeated the word to himself.

He understood her perfectly. Since he joined the Missionary school, he had been taught to pray. And especially the pupils were made to recite 'The Lord's Prayer' and some other religious recitations at certain periods during schooling hours every day, since the school was established by Catholic missionaries. He only understood this to be the western way of communicating with God. At home, he never prayed.

Mary went on to explain to him that prayer was a personal way of communicating with God. It was more than biblical recitations. She first had to clarify that there were different ways by which people prayed to God, and she equally enlightened Okiki that the Catholic missionaries' way of praying was learnt from some God's peculiar nation. She taught Okiki how to kneel down every morning and night, and communicate with the Unseen One. She also explained that faith in God was an essential ingredient in getting answers to one's prayers. And if he believed that God rewards all those who seek Him, his prayers would be answered too.

"You can teach your mother how to pray too." Mary suggested further.

Okiki's spirit bubbled under the news. He was excited to know that God was for all tribe and races. And that if he sought Him diligently, his heart's desires would be fulfilled too. Mary had also added that prayer was Joseph's key to moving from the prison to the palace. Okiki wanted to be as great as that biblical Joseph. And now that he had the key, he would surely use it daily.

"Did you receive any news from your friend in the city?" Okiki asked afterwards.

Mary knew the smart boy was indirectly asking if she received any news about his elder brother's return to the village. Mary made a jocular remark about how two love birds stuck to each other, and they laughed loudly under the afternoon breeze. And they teased one another over how the two young couples enjoyed each other's company in the city.

Amope had seen her little son kneeling down, facing the wall at the corner of his room, and talking in low tones to someone he did not see, with his eyes shut. She caught him doing this every day and night. At first she ignored this ritual, but as the days went by, she begged Okiki for some understanding.

Okiki's charm had worked. He knew if he had first advised his mother to pray, she might not agree since their traditional way of worshipping God was quite different. Although none of them in the family practised the traditional religion of worshipping deities. But they consulted mediums occasionally, and observed peace offerings. Amope's heart gladly received her little boy's opinion on God. And from that moment onward, they prayed every day and night.

As each day and night went by, life became more unbearable for Jomi in the city. Doja made life unbearable for her. He easily lost his temper over every flimsy issue, and he never hesitated to express his anger towards her. Jomi's plea for peace and understanding fell on deaf ears, and often stoked the fire of anger on Doja's mind.

A once sweet relationship had now turned sour. Doja's hatred had first begun for his job, and he always transferred his aggression on Jomi. He wanted another job, and Jomi would not agree to this. She begged him to be reasonable, and also give her some time to get him a better job. Doja was losing his patience, and he believed Jomi was not trying at all. He soon stopped eating her food, and her presence bored him.

"If there is anything I have done to make you suddenly dislike me, tell me and I would amend my ways," Jomi begged, on a particular weekend.

Doja was seated on the sofa, and Jomi crawled towards him on her knees. He rebuffed her request, and quietly advised her not to get closer to him, or touch him. This had been on for long, and Jomi saw this as a great torture for her. She wanted it to stop. And she wanted them to return back to the happy times they once shared together. She defied his orders, and audaciously moved towards him, and leaned on his laps.

Doja was furious. He pushed her away, and the young woman lost balance and hit her head against the floor. Jomi began to weep. And Doja went on shouting at the top of his voice; threatening to kill her if she dared to touch him again. Suddenly, Jomi felt an unusual movement in her womb. Her eyes rolled and her sight seemed to become blurry, and she felt an irritation around her throat. She jumped up and ran to the toilet to vomit.

"What is wrong?" Doja enquired, as he appeared behind her.

Jomi became reluctant to talk. That was not the first time she vomited. And over the past few weeks she had felt a sudden heaviness in her nature. And she was losing taste for food too. She did not have fever. She was sure what it was.

"I am pregnant." She replied gently.

Doja did not believe his ears. He was going to become a father. They stared at each other blankly.

——11——

Another Carved Tom-Tom

S HE SUFFERED A miscarriage. Debisi was lying helpless on the floor when she saw her wrapper was stained with blood and her legs were sticky. Warm blood flowed freely down her thighs. She burst into loud cries.

Kasali stood over her without pity. He felt no remorse for his second wife. Earlier that afternoon, Debisi had gone to ask Kasali for her feeding allowance. And a reckless shove was the reply she got from him. The fragile pregnant woman was sent reeling backwards, and she hit her belly against the walls of the hut before eventually falling down.

Kasali hissed at her, and walked out of the hut angrily. Debisi writhed in pains.

Debisi's travails in Kasali's house knew no bounds. Ever before she had to lose her unborn child that way, her future was already in jeopardy and her life was losing direction. Kasali's behaviour towards her was always rash and unkind. He neither gave her attention nor care. And every night, when he came to meet her, he ravaged her body like a starving beast.

Asake became envious of Debisi, since her husband preferred to spend the night with the younger wife. And she never hesitated to transfer her aggression on Debisi. She made the young woman do all the house chores; travel long distances to fetch water from the village well, and also send her to and from the market as many times as possible. Okiki had visited his sister twice, and met her in such an uncomfortable condition, and Debisi had begged him not to tell their mother. She believed Amope's knowledge of her domestic challenges would not make any difference, rather it could spell more trouble for her, and worrying could make Amope's health deteriorate too.

Debisi's pregnancy made things worse. Asake was displeased. And she did not hide her grievances. Debisi's domestic tasks were doubled, and life became more unbearable for her. Kasali had also seen how Asake maltreated his younger wife, but he never rebuked Asake. Debisi did not have a say in the house. She was treated like a slave. And she succumbed meekly. But the burden was indeed telling on her. Each day brought her unending tasks and pains, and each night was filled with torture. The young woman feared her life was already taking after her mothers'. She cried to herself.

Amope ran all the way from her hut down to Kasali's hut. Okiki followed swiftly behind her, bringing Amope's scarf and slippers which she had hurriedly left behind. It was some kind neighbours who had come to share the bad news. Amope could not hold back her feelings, she wailed loudly when she saw her daughter's condition. Debisi was still on the floor, writhing in pains.

"Mother, I have lost my child." Debisi groaned.

The response Debisi got from her mother was loud cries. Okiki was also saddened by his sister's condition. He loved her dearly, they were bosom friends, and he never wished her life would turn out this way. Okiki cried too. Amope panted up and down the hut, she was confused, not knowing what to do. But some kind neighbours, who had also heard about the sudden mishap, had equally showed up in Kasali's hut to offer some assistance.

"Let us take her to the midwife's house quickly." One of them suggested.

Asake who witnessed how it all happened, and had offered no assistance to salvage Debisi's life, now hid in her room. She feared if the neighbours and Amope knew she was at home and had showed coldness about it all, they could tear her into pieces. From the corner of her dark room, she watched as they all helped Debisi clean up the blood stains; wash her face, before taking her to the popular midwife's house.

Kasali did not show up at the midwife's house until two days after the incident. Amope was very furious, and she did not hide her feelings.

"You are such a heartless man!" Amope yelled.

"Woman, don't talk to me that way." Kasali snapped back.

His cruel response fuelled Amope's anger towards him. The midwife had gone out to get some medicinal herbs, when Kasali showed up. Debisi who lay down asleep in the corner of the hut was awakened by the altercation. Okiki sat at the edge of his sister's mat, and watched as his mother challenged Kasali. He was glad she did.

"How do you expect me to talk to you? Did I give you my daughter so that you could be maltreating her?" Amope challenged.

"You dare not challenge how I treat my wife. Did I steal her from your hut?" Kasali bellowed.

Amope was totally disappointed by the way Kasali spoke. He proved himself to be a wolf in sheep's skin. He was no human in any way. She could now see clearly that all he did for her was just a ploy to get her daughter.

"As soon as my daughter recovers fully, am taking her back home."

"You dare not, you ingrate!!!" Kasali snapped back, and stormed out of the midwife's hut.

A sudden contraction of Amope's nerves was felt as soon as Kasali left the hut. Kasali's last words rang through her brain. Amope sank her buttocks on a low stool, and sealed her lips. She had been caught in a trap. Kasali would make his threat true, if she attempted to take Debisi back to her hut. Amope shook her head violently, and blamed herself for her daughter's misfortune. The poor widow cried silently.

It was when her waters broke that it finally dawned on Doja that his future would be reflected in the eyes of his child. The past eight months had been very uncomfortable for him. His worries increased as his wife's tummy protruded. His usual complaint and anger waned with the months, but he was more concerned with how to cater for a child they did not prepare for. Deep down his mind, he felt Jomi had purposely gone pregnant to bait him. But he did not say a word about it, he just kept to himself.

Jomi had gone through the burden all by herself. Doja had shown little care about her pregnancy, but at least, she was happy he was conscious of his behaviour towards her, and they never had a cause to quarrel again. The beautiful woman saved all her money, and also bought everything she would need for her delivery in advance.

Jomi stopped working when her pregnancy was seven months old. She knew her chances of retaining her job were slim; since it was not stated in her employment records that she was married. This pregnancy was turning out to be a stain on her career. But she never felt this way. The joy of becoming a mother filled her heart. And the idea that she was going to bear her child for the only man she had loved all her life brought her so much joy.

They refused to talk to each other about the pregnancy. They went through their daily routines, as if nothing had changed. Doja knew Jomi must have had a lot going through her mind, and the pregnancy would have been giving her pains she refused to talk about. A feeling of guilt swept over him as each month went by. He was now embarrassed by the nonchalant attitude he had shown over the past few months. But still, he was too proud to get off his high horse.

He suddenly fell off his high horse when her waters broke. He was relaxing at the balcony that Saturday morning when Jomi called out for help. He rushed inside to get her things, and with a kind neighbour's car, they got his wife to the hospital.

Doja paced up and down the hospital reception, as he awaited the delivery of their first child. He was filled with nostalgia as he awaited the good news. He remembered the childhood years he once spent with Jomi. He also remembered how she disappeared from Irewolu village, and how fate had brought them together again. He realised how unfit he was for the educated and beautiful young lady. And he could not ignore how she had wrapped her arms of love around him and erased every difference between them.

Jomi had stuck by him through thick and thin. She had proved herself not just as a suitable companion, but also as a mother too. Doja realised her virtues towered above his' in all standard. And he now regretted all his insincere and ungrateful actions towards her. He had been impatient, intolerable, and unreasonable in most situations. At that point, Doja realised he had always been a selfish man. He clasped his hands over his mouth, and he prayed silently for the safe delivery of his wife, as his eyes were dampened with tears.

The tears that once coagulated above his eyes now trickled down his face as he beheld the face of his first child. He shed tears of joy as he beheld the beautiful child in the cot. Words could not describe how happy he felt that day. Doja's faced beamed with happiness. He was glad to be a father.

Jomi had gone through a rigorous moment before giving birth to their first child later in the afternoon of that glorious Saturday. She was allowed to rest for a short while after the delivery. Her joy also knew no bounds. She was happy to be a mother too. But she wondered how Doja must have been feeling.

Doja walked into the maternity ward. He was delighted to see the radiance in his wife's eyes. Jomi lay sweetly on the bed, and Doja sat gently at the edge, close to her. They looked into each other's eyes. But they did not say a word to each other. Doja held her right palm tenderly. And he gently wiped the sweat off her forehead with the other hand. Jomi blushed. And they both giggled nervously as they looked at each other. They were proud to become parents. They both knew a child with the symbolism of love had been born. They now had a baby girl.

Amope was restless that Saturday morning too. Okiki watched her move up and down the hut. It had been many weeks since Debisi returned to Kasali's hut. Amope was not happy about it. But she was left with no other option. Okiki took up the duty of visiting his sister once every week. And he always came back with a reasonable report. Amope knew everything Okiki reported about his sister's welfare wasn't true. And she knew it was a joint agreement between Debisi and Okiki. Whether she liked it or not, Amope understood she had failed as a mother and her selfish decision had wrecked her daughter's happiness. She knew how miserable Debisi must be feeling in Kasali's house, and she silently hoped for better days to come.

Okiki also understood how his mother had been feeling over the past few weeks. And he was encouraged by the way she prayed silently and faithfully to God every day. But that Saturday morning was different. Okiki wondered what could have gone wrong.

"Mother, what is wrong?" The young boy asked.

"I have a feeling Doja is going through a difficult moment." She replied briskly.

Okiki laughed shortly. But he did not laugh loud enough for his mother to hear. He wondered where she got the feeling from. His brother had left them about two years back and it was just now that his mother felt he was in trouble. Moreover, Doja was several kilometres away.

"Mother, how are you so sure about that?" Okiki teased.

"He is my son, and he sucked my breasts . . . ."

Okiki listened as his mother went on narrating that there is a motherly intuition that all African mothers felt about their children, whenever something was wrong with any of them. Okiki listened as his mother explained that once the child sucks their mother's breasts, there seem to be a spiritual bond of love between the mother and her children, even if distance separates them both.

"So what do you think is wrong with him?"

Okiki had actually wanted to ask if his mother hadn't been missing Doja, and was longing to see him again. But he felt that question would have peeled off scabs of old wounds in his mother's heart. So he twisted it.

"I can't really say. But I can feel his heart is troubled." The dear widow replied.

"I suggest we should pray." Okiki suggested.

Amope saw it as a bright idea. Ever since her little son taught her to always make her requests known to her Creator through prayers, she had been enjoying a certain relief since then. Since they were the only ones in their hut, they shut their eyes and prayed for Doja immediately.

Mother and son later opened their eyes only to gaze some familiar faces standing in the hut. It was a robust woman in her late thirties, with her two children; a boy and a girl. The children were twins, and Okiki knew them. The twins were a few years younger than Okiki, but their mother was much younger than Amope. Amope recognised her as the food seller at the village square, and they both shared a decent relationship with one another in the village. The woman knelt down and greeted Amope, as Okiki found a stool for her and her children to sit.

"Please, Amope I need the help of your son, Okiki." The woman started.

Okiki was startled when his name was mentioned. Even Amope was surprised too. Mother and son wondered what help they had in store. The woman went on to explain how she admired as Okiki went to school in the neighbouring village. And she was proud Amope had supported such a noble intention; since her son was the first to do so in their village. She said she had been hearing good reports about Okiki's brilliance, and she wanted her children to also receive the western education.

Okiki and his mother were thrilled to their toes. This was the first time they received positive news about their family. Moreover, Okiki was delighted to know that the bright light of education was already reflecting into his village through him. As seasons and sessions went by, he had always hoped that someday he would enlighten his people about the values of education. But he did not know how to do it. He feared being rejected and rebuked by his villagers. He knew this was his chance, and he was not going to lose it.

"Yes, your children can. A new session begins in three months time." Okiki replied delightfully.

"But do you think my children can learn the western knowledge?" The woman queried.

"Yes, they can." Okiki replied affirmatively.

"What about my daughter," The woman asked, pointing to the feminine twin, "do you think she also has the brains for it?"

"Yes, she can. Everyone can." Okiki replied in laughter.

He wondered why the woman felt her daughter could not assimilate or comprehend what was taught at school. Moreover, there were female students at school too. Even his teacher, Mary, was once a student, and now a brilliant and admirable intelligentsia. But Amope could understand the woman's fears. She had once felt that way to. So she came up with a bright idea.

"I suggest Okiki should take them through some of his first school lessons, for the next two months. And if your children find it comprehensible they can enrol into the school in the coming session."

Okiki and the woman saw this as a brilliant idea. Okiki said he would be willing to tutor them, thrice in a week for an hour each. And he assured the woman that her children would find education a great delight, as they would become the first set of twins from Irewolu village to do so. They all roared with laughter. The pleasant woman offered to pay Okiki a weekly stipend for his act of generosity, but he declined the offer. Mother and son smiled at each other, knowing fame was already knocking on their door.

Doja realised how fragile, and yet invaluable life seemed when he carried his baby girl in his hands. He watched as she looked at him through her tiny eyes. And her smile made him shudder with excitement. The thoughts of childhood flitted across his mind. He had once been a child too. And he had equally been nurtured in the cradle of his mother, and led by the hands of his father.

He suddenly realised how much his mother's love meant to him. And he also understood why his father's arrogance could not make them come to terms with each other. They had both nurtured him, and truly in many instances, they knew better than him. Even if they had their lapses, he was supposed to correct them with soberness and respect. Fighting his father wasn't the best solution; fleeing from the village made no difference either. Doja realised he had offended his mother greatly. He wondered how the poor widow must be feeling by now.

The arrival of his baby girl gave him many reasons to reflect upon his life. He was her mirror. He had gone through a kind of parenting he would never want his daughter to experience. Doja was ready to be a better person; a great role model for his daughter. If these desires were to come true, he needed to retrace his steps and right his wrongs as soon as he could.

"I have a confession to make." Doja blurted out.

It was a smooth Sunday evening, and the young couples were peaceful seated in their living room. The birth of their daughter had moistened their relationship, and cemented their love. Since they returned back from the hospital, Doja had apologised to his wife for his misdemeanours and oversight. He explained to his dutiful wife that he had been under much pressure in the years past and had been trying to pick the pieces of his life together. He promised to love her through the years of abundance, and also hold her tight through the stormy nights.

And ever since then, they had been spending long hours together. Doja always hurried back home to see his wife and daughter. And they took turns to look after their baby at midnight. Jomi was pleased Doja had become a better person. He had changed completely within the few days they returned back from the hospital. His behaviour was now humane and sincere. He became the once loving man she knew him to be. She was happy. She wondered what confession he had to make that evening.

"Am all ears," Jomi replied calmly.

Jomi was shocked as Doja revealed that his mother and siblings did not know his whereabouts till the moment he was speaking. He revealed to his wife that he had fled from the village because the villagers had been pointing accusing fingers at him.

Jomi was greatly disappointed and saddened by the confession. A myriad of revelations dashed across her mind. She now realised why Doja refused to talk about his family, and was always brutish whenever she raised the idea of visiting the village. She wondered what Amope must have gone through over the past years. And she greatly feared if Okiki's education had not stopped. She just could not imagine what must have happened to Doja's only sister, Debisi. At first, Jomi's facial expression was bitter, but she quickly brushed it off with a sigh.

She loved Doja with all his faults. And she understood that his confession showed that he had repented from his mistakes. And as such, they now had to focus on how to rebuild the broken image. He needed help that was why he confessed everything. And she was ready to stand by him.

"We have to return to the village." Jomi retorted, after much silence.

"Yes, am ready." Doja replied calmly.

Jomi's face broke into a smile. And Doja dabbed his eyes.

—12—

Somebody Lied

MARY LISTENED WITH rapt attention, as Okiki told her about his exploits in his village. The young boy was fast becoming a force to reckon with in his village. The tri-weekly tutorial had first started with the twins. But within the last two months it had later increased into a team of five potential students, consisting of four boys and a girl.

Mary was really impressed by Okiki's zeal and tenacity. The young boy had shown so much courage and determination towards bringing the light of education to his village, in spite of his own academic workload. Despite his domestic incapacity, Okiki had still been able to shoulder the weight of five ignorant children. Mary was also quick to remember Okiki had just turned eleven years.

They had just concluded their promotional exams. And Okiki had not only promoted to the final year at the primary school, but his results had remained at the top spot too, while his colleagues struggled behind him. Mary was now convinced Okiki would set a brilliant record for himself, his family, his village and the school, by excelling at the scholarship exams. His performance over the years had shown that he merited the scholarship. And Mary believed all her efforts on Okiki would not go in vain.

"I will be bringing my friends to the school for their enrolment during the holiday." Okiki added.

Mary admired as he spoke. Her face broke into a bright smile. She could still remember when her friend, Jomi, brought the little village boy to the school five years back. And now the same boy had grown into a young chap, who now brings some of his village subordinates to school too. She marvelled at how the significance of education could not be undermined.

But Mary had a little burden eating her up inside. It had been giving her sleepless nights. She was about to make a decision that would likely severe her relationship with her best friend. Normally, Mary was supposed to have made positive and encouraging remarks to all Okiki had been saying. But instead she just smiled at him. Okiki did not notice. He was carried away by his personal excitement. She had to tell Okiki about it. But she knew that day was not the best day for such issues. She remained quiet about it.

On his way back home, Okiki stopped by to have a long chat with the cashew tree. He looked around the branches in search of fruits. But the cashew tree was out of season; its leaves partly withered, and there were no fruits on it. He missed the sweet cashew fruits. He had often plucked some on his way to school. And his classmates scrambled over one another to have a taste of the fruit. Some of them even rumoured it was the source of Okiki's extraordinary brilliance.

"Just as you are looking all around me in search of fruits, someday the world would reckon with you, and they would not make decisions until they find you." The cashew tree spoke.

Okiki did not want to believe what he heard. Truly, that afternoon, Okiki was feeling on top of the world because he was moving to his final year at the primary school. But what the cashew tree just said was beyond his imagination. He saw himself as a mere village boy who simply wanted to get a brilliant life, and use it to save his family, and probably develop his village too.

Even at that, such a dream was way beyond him. His little education had taught him that the world consisted of billions of people from different races, tribes and continents. Moreover, the pace at which the world was moving was just too fast for him to fit in. All he wanted was to be a good role model and earn a decent living.

"The world moves in circles. If you look at the edges of the circle, you might be consumed by its vastness. But if you could find your way to the centre, then you could truly have the world at your fingertips." The cashew tree explained further, after listening to Okiki's thoughts.

"How do I get to the centre?" Okiki enquired.

He did not need to ask how the mysterious tree read his mind; the experience over the years had made it a normal phenomenon. The whole idea of becoming reckoned by the world was beginning to make much meaning to him. He had earlier been viewing the edges of the world, now he wanted to see what existed or made up the centre of the world.

"The centre is made up of the best people in the world. And you just have to make being the best your goal in life. Pursue your dreams diligently. Be the best at what you do. And someday, you might be at the centre." The cashew tree explained expressly.

Okiki just could not fathom the depth of the cashew tree's understanding about life. Everything was now making so much sense to him. But the curious young boy wasn't satisfied yet, he pressed further.

"Is there a particular vocation or dream that those at the centre all share?"

After hearing the young boy's question, the cashew tree burst into a loud roar of laughter. Okiki did not like such. He often felt stupid and embarrassed whenever the cashew tree laughed over his questions. But he remained calm. The cashew tree's intentional laughter would not distract him from learning this priceless truth.

"If you spend your life trying to be like someone, you might end up living in that person's shadow." That was the first truth the mysterious tree clarified to the young boy.

"The people at the centre shared a common habit, common dream, and common skill: Excellence, Big dreams, and going the extra-mile." The cashew tree had to still expatiate further having seen that the young boy was still confused by what was just said.

"You must have big dreams first, show excellence in your dreams, and go the extra-mile to show that you truly deserve to be at the centre." The cashew tree concluded, and gave the young boy some time to ruminate over all it just said.

Okiki realised that all humans had different dreams in life. But the underlining word was that the people at the centre dreamt bigger than the rest. They pursued that dream excellently, just to prove that they were the best at whatever they did. And they all went the extra-mile to ensure that their dreams were achieved, since the road to the centre must have been discouraging and full of adversities that could choke up their dreams. Okiki understood it all. And the words of the cashew tree struck a chord in him, and he knew he belonged to the centre.

"Time is the essential ingredient you need to perfect your dreams, while opportunity is the spell that will turn your dreams into reality someday." The cashew tree advised.

"*Time* and *Opportunity*," Okiki repeated the two words.

"Yes, the two. Make time your most suitable companion, and let opportunity be the Golden Fleece you will always search for."

Okiki breathed in heavily, and allowed the fresh breath of to air clear his lungs. A vista of opportunities spanned across his eyes. And he could see that what life had in store for him was greater than he could imagine. He understood the journey was going to be rough, but he was ready to paint a great picture of his life. He turned to leave.

"You don't need me to fulfil your dreams. Neither do you need your loved ones to fulfil them. Your persistent desire to succeed will make a way for you."

Okiki could hear the cashew tree's last words at the back of his ears, as he left. His life was wrapped around the cashew tree and his loved ones, and there was no way he could do without them. They meant a lot to him. Moreover that was why he lived. He ignored the last advice.

The holiday had turned out to be the most pleasant for Okiki. He spent his days reading in preparatory for his last year at the primary school. He offered assistance to his mother in every way she required. He also did not fail to check on his sister's welfare, despite hearing the same ugly news every time. And he did not fail to prepare his potential students for the schooling days ahead.

Okiki's students had also shown great agility for brilliance. And he was proud of them. They also went the extra mile in assisting him with his farm work whenever they were indisposed. And their mothers had equally sent food items to Amope as their way of gratitude. Everything was going on well, and both mother and son were pleased.

But an evening changed a whole lot of things. Scabs of old wounds were peeled off. The fetish spirits of deliverance refused to be appeased. And some haunting memories were awakened. Okiki's students had just left their hut a few moments back, and Amope was about preparing their supper when suddenly she felt a surge within her bowels. Okiki took a quick glance at his dear mother, and saw that she was turning pale. Before he could hurry to grab her, Amope's bones stiffened, her legs twisted together, and she slumped on the harsh sands at the backyard of the hut.

Okiki cried for help as his mother was thrown into an epilepsy fit. Okiki ran idly around Amope, as the helpless poor widow rolled and twisted violently on the hard ground. Okiki could not touch her, and the idea of running to his sister for help might be just too late. Amope's nerves became taut, and her eyes bulged. Okiki screamed as his mother began to foam at the mouth. The fit later subsided, Amope's eyes rolled upwards, and she had become totally pale as she lay still.

The poor boy slumped to his knees, and began to cry. He dug his head in the sands and wailed. His mind was in total turmoil. His mother's sickness had returned. And the cobra's head that they thought had been buried had finally been dug out of the soil again. Okiki could sense an impending danger was imminent.

Amope sat on a low stool several minutes after the incident occurred. Okiki had helped her up after a fresh breeze blew over her. Okiki had remained silent, as Amope walk awkwardly into the hut to have her bath. And now she was sitting at the backyard, talking to herself, but saying nothing. The poor widow felt the epilepsy fit she just went through had pulled on the chord of her life. She saw visions of afterlife. And she could feel her body and bones were already betraying her. And she might not have the strength to go through such pain and agony again.

"My life has been miserable." Amope spoke out, as fresh tears brewed over her eyes.

"Mother, don't say that." Okiki cried.

"As much as you care for everyone you meet in life, you have cared for me." Amope spoke again in garbled manner.

"Mother, I don't understand." Okiki begged.

The young boy was getting scared. Amope's discordant utterances worried Okiki. The way she gaped into the dark night made Okiki feeble and lonely. Amope stood up, and went inside to sleep. Okiki just swallowed a cup of bitterness. He was not hungry any more. He followed his mother meekly, and slept beside her. That night, Okiki snuggled up to his mother, closer than ever before.

It was loud and forceful knocks on the door that forced Kasali and his family out of their dreams. They all wondered who might be at the door at the dawn of the day. Kasali led the way and others remained in their rooms, as the intense rapping on the door continued. He opened the door slowly, to see who was behind it.

Amope pushed him backwards, and stormed into Kasali's hut. Okiki quickly hurried in behind her. Amope's presence in his hut greatly infuriated him. But he was caught unaware, and did not know what was going on.

"I want to have my daughter back." Amope yelled, as she scampered around the hut in search of Debisi.

"You will do no such thing!" Kasali retorted and pulled her back.

"Did you pay for her bride price? Didn't you just trick me to have my daughter?" Amope bellowed.

Debisi had heard her dear mother's voice. She rushed out of her room to meet her, but was stopped by Kasali's angry looks. Asake and her children kept their distance, and watched from a corner of the hut.

"You are an ingrate! Is this how you intend to repay me after saving your life?" Kasali snapped back.

"You are a liar. All you and your native doctor did was just a hoax to get at me and my daughter. You knew all along that there was no cure for my sickness!" Amope screamed at the top of her voice, pointing a finger at Kasali's nose, as bitter tears wet her face.

"But at least it alleviated your epilepsy crisis. So get out of my house."

Kasali's harsh response provoked Amope. Okiki's jaws dropped as new revelations were revealed before him and his sister. He wondered how his mother knew Kasali had tricked them. He did not understand how she became so certain overnight that Kasali and the native doctor knew there was no cure for her sickness. But Kasali's unkind response proved he had planned it all along, and was already prepared for this day.

"You are a wicked soul!!" Amope exclaimed, and ran towards Kasali.

Kasali pushed her back, and was quickly propped back to her feet by Okiki. Debisi cried, as she realised she had been pawned all along. Okiki was furious too, but the altercation just wasn't the best measure. He held his mother's hands, and drew her gently out of Kasali's hut.

Amope cried all the way back to her hut. The day had already matured into its full bloom by then, and every villager they met on the way wondered what was wrong with Amope. The poor widow pulled at her hair, and cursed herself, as she wailed. Okiki's pleas could not assuage her feelings. Even the young boy needed someone to comfort him too.

The arrival of Doja, Jomi and their baby into Amope's hut was embraced by emptiness. Their excitement had waned when they met no one in the hut. Jomi went back outside to make enquiries from neighbours. Doja searched around; his place of birth had not changed much. The rough clay walls, the thatch ceiling, and the moist atmosphere was almost the same way he had left it. Doja was indeed excited to be home again, but the absence of his mother and siblings gave him much concern.

Since his disappearance, much rain had created gullies around the village paths. And he wondered if the flood hadn't swept away his family. He bit his lower lips. Jomi came back in to inform him that a neighbour said they had seen Amope and Okiki go out at dawn. Doja's mind rested a bit, as they awaited their peaceful return.

It was Okiki that first caught sight of two adults waiting in front of their hut. Amope's eyes were still crumpled in tears, and did not see anything. Okiki took a closer look at them; he had seen a young man and a young woman with a child strapped to her back. A quick recognition of his elder brother tore a big smile on his face. He shouted for joy and ran towards the hut.

Amope had heard Okiki mention his brother's name. She looked ahead, and hurriedly wiped her face with the edge of her wrapper. It was true; Amope did not believe her eyes. Her first child was waiting in front of her hut. The poor widow knew God had surely remembered her, and answered her lonely prayers. A day that had started badly a while ago, now seem to be a fulfilment to all her dreams. She rushed forward.

Doja caught his mother midway. And they held each other in a long, tearful embrace. Different memories flashed across each mind, and they allowed their thoughts to swim through it all. Okiki was also excited to see Jomi again, and he was most delighted to know she now had a child too. Her effervescent beauty was without compare, and Okiki was proud his elder brother had made the right choice. She was the instrument God used for his academic enlightenment. And he knew he was eternally indebted to her. Okiki had a lot of experiences he wanted to share with her.

"Mother, I am so sorry." Doja apologised.

They had all settled down in the hut. And Doja prostrated on the floor before his mother. Jomi knelt beside her husband, pleading with her mother-in-law. Okiki sat close to Amope, and took a detailed look at his brother. Doja had changed; his once varicose veins that ran across his skin, was now hidden beneath a pile of glittering skin. His rough moustache had now recoiled into a smooth elegance. The young boy knew his mother equally admired his elder brother, and bore no grudge against him, so he did not interfere. Amope hurriedly pulled Jomi back to her feet. And she drew her first son closer to her bosom. Her joy knew no bounds that morning, and she could not find any place in her heart where she bore a grudge towards her son.

Time had its way of eclipsing the events of life. They spent the next few hours talking about all that had happened while they were apart. Amope talked about how they had been surviving while he was away, and had excited Doja and Jomi's feelings when she told them about Okiki's academic exploits. Doja was impressed, and he also talked about how he now earned a decent salary in the city, and would be able to afford to send Okiki to a secondary school in the city. Their joy and laughter flitted on the walls of the hut, as they all rejoiced over the new born.

"Where is Debisi?"

Doja was later forced to ask, when he observed that the minutes went by and she was far from sight, and neither did they mention anything about her. Amope's countenance became morose, and she avoided Doja's inquisitive gaze. Doja could easily tell something was totally wrong. And no one was ready to tell him. Jomi held his palms, and fiddled with it.

"I will explain everything to you brother." Okiki voiced out.

Doja was surprised to hear Okiki speak. His once little brother, had now grown into a vocal young man. He held still, and listened attentively. Okiki calmly explained how Debisi's life had been pawned in the quest to salvage Amope's life; only for them to now realise Kasali had tricked them after all. Doja clenched his fists and gnashed his teeth to hold back his anger. He realised his absence had caused a lot of damage, and he regretted his actions. For many minutes after Okiki concluded, the hut was silent, and they all avoided each other's gaze.

"Get up, Okiki. We are going to bring home Debisi." Doja spoke calmly.

His tone was calm, and he was well comported as he stood up. Jomi and Amope stared at each other, as they feared Doja might harm Kasali. Their lips remained sealed, as Okiki and Doja walked out of the hut.

Debisi had remained at a corner in the hut crying, since her mother left. She felt her future had been marred. And she would have to spend the rest of her life in misery and pain. Kasali had remained defiant in the hut, expecting

Amope might return with strong youths in the village that could help her kidnap her daughter from his house. Asake sang insulting songs targeted at Debisi and Kasali as she moved around the house, after discovering what the whole truth was.

A wind of change suddenly blew into the hut. Kasali shuddered on his seat as Doja walked into his hut. He could not believe his eyes. Debisi's eyes lit with total surprise, as her elder brother walked in. She was stultified.

"Debisi, get up and let's go home." Doja spoke firmly.

Kasali caught the baleful look in Doja's eyes, as he ordered. The spear-head of their house had returned. And the reports Kasali knew about him made him weak to his knees. Debisi sprang to her feet, and ran to join her long lost brother. Debisi led the way out of Kasali's compound, Okiki followed, and Doja was the last to leave.

Debisi did not pick a thing as she left Kasali's house for good.

—13—

Tears of the Lonely

OKIKI GOT HIS first shock when he resumed back
in school. The fresh breeze surreptitiously oozed
around the school compound. Okiki breathed and sighed
with delight. He was glad to be back in school. Most
importantly, he was in the final year.

But the excitement quickly waned, when a dark,
grotesque looking, short baldy man stepped into
the classroom and introduced himself as their new
class-teacher. All the students were caught in a web of
surprise. Okiki was equally dumbfounded. He searched
for Mary throughout the school during break time. But
she was nowhere to be found, and there was no particular

information about her disappearance from anyone. The first day at school, turned sour for Okiki. His mind was lost.

The sun pressed like a boulder on his head, as he walked back home later in the afternoon. His heart was bleak and desolate. He could not imagine why Mary had suddenly disappeared without a friendly notice. Mostly, he blamed himself for the years they had spent together without knowing where she resided in Kajola village. His eyes were clouded with tears. A tinge of anger dangled over his thought, as he bit his nails listlessly.

Like a hazy image vanishes and reappears, Okiki could see a lissom figure standing afar off. He could see a lady waiting by the road. He wished the person was his doting class-teacher. And his imagination turned to reality, when Mary called out his name.

"Okiki, hurry up, have been waiting for you."

Truly, it was Mary. Okiki could not believe his eyes. A bird fluttered in his belly. He was overexcited. He ran towards her, and she caught him in a swinging embrace. They did not say a word to each other, until they reached their meeting place; beneath the acacia tree, on the hill.

"I would be travelling to England in two days time." Mary broke the silence.

Okiki did not say a word. He had heard about England before. The villagers often called it 'The King's Country'. There were so many fantasies shared about England amongst the villagers, and one was that people no longer went by sea, but could now travel there through a vehicle that flew in the air. Rumour also had it that England was a land of wealth and greatness. Anyone who went there would be successful. Okiki had many of such fantasies in his mind that he could now confirm from his doting friend, but the circumstances around him did not allow him to do such. He remained quiet.

Mary went on explaining that she would be receiving her university education in one of the schools in England. And she may not come back until five years time. Tears trickled down her face, as she told Okiki she might not see him again. Okiki did not cry. Somehow, he felt a strong conviction in him that Mary's purpose in his life had been completed. And he must let her go, and also wish her well in her sojourn in life. But still, he did not say a word.

The two friends got up, and walked down the hill silently. Okiki's eyes were laced with tears. For the first time, he could feel his heart was broken. At the crossroads, Okiki eventually voiced out. He did not say much. All he did was to show gratitude for Mary's kindness, support and generosity towards him, and he promised not to let her down. They held each other in a long embrace, before eventually parting ways. Mary wiped her tears, as she walked away from Okiki. They were tears of joy. She had once lost a younger brother to the cold hands of death, but now she would be losing another one to the uncertain hands of time.

Okiki walked home silently. His lips were heavy with tears. So he kept them closed. He did not know this was the way he would end his relationship with Mary. He had a lot of good things in his mind that he wanted to share with her. He wanted to say much about the happy reunion in his family. But time had a way of changing things. He sighed.

"Great people have a way of finding each other. If you stay on the path of greatness, you would surely meet again." The cashew tree spoke calmly.

Okiki stopped. He was just about to pass by the cashew tree, when he heard what the cashew tree said, loudly. He looked at the tree, he wanted to talk, but his lips quivered. He sniffled back to hold the tears. And he walked home.

The subsequent weeks in Amope's hut had brought so much joy. The small family sat together and discussed a way out of their dilemma. Doja had learnt his lessons, and had grown to become a wiser and stronger person. They all watched as he proffered solutions to the family problems.

He first reiterated his intention to send Okiki to school in the city, as soon as he receives his primary school results, even if he did not merit the scholarship. He also suggested that Debisi would be brought down to the city, as soon as they can help her secure a decent job. So that she can wipe away the bitter memories and start her life afresh in a better place. He finally suggested that Amope be taken down to the city urgently for medical attention concerning her sickness.

Amope and the other children saw this as a great idea, but the poor widow insisted she would wait till Okiki concluded his primary education, before going to the city.

Doja felt this was not plausible, because from the news he received, Amope's health was growing worse, and the idea of waiting for a long duration of nine months for Okiki to conclude his school was not advisable and risky too.

Truly, Amope did not want to leave her last child alone at this moment when he needed her most. Moreover, Doja was just starting a family of his own, and he needed some time to put things in order. So that the family burden and expenses would not break him down or affect his marriage. The next nine months would be good for him to stabilize things. Doja persuaded her to change her mind, but Amope insisted. The matter was concluded peacefully, and Doja agreed to return to the village as soon as Okiki concluded his final exams.

Okiki drew into his own world of loneliness, as he thought about his beloved class-teacher's sudden departure. He also rejoiced with his elder brother, as Doja formalised his traditional marriage with his beautiful wife. Amope was the happiest person on that day. Although, the marriage had been done in such a quiet and modest manner, Amope was glad his son had found a rare gem. And she was most hopeful, because she had lived to see her son start a better generation she had only dreamed of. Amope teased at the marriage ceremony that if she died afterwards, she would have died in peace.

It was the week that Doja and his family returned back to the city that Okiki got the greatest shock of his life. Apparently, he often went to school every morning with the other five students from the village. Although, they were in their first year at school and also younger than Okiki, but going to school together in the morning was fun for all. They chatted about the previous day's event, and also sought Okiki's advice on many issues. Okiki enjoyed their company, and the long journey to school suddenly became a short one. But Okiki never returns home with the five younger students. He always spent an extra hour at school in preparatory for his final exams. And walking back home alone later in the afternoon was a privacy he enjoyed.

But that morning was different. Okiki felt a cold rush, as he passed by the cashew tree. The breeze around that spot was chilling. He took a glance at the position of the cashew tree; he did not see a thing. But the younger friends surrounding him to school that morning enveloped his attention. So he passed.

On his way back home in the afternoon, he had actually passed by the cashew tree before he halted. Something was missing. He looked at the position where the cashew tree stood, and all he could see were the innards of the bush that surrounded the mysterious tree. Like a magic wand conjures images to vanish and reappear, Okiki felt the mysterious tree had disappeared, or become transparent. But the cashew tree was no more there.

Okiki held his breath when he looked downwards. The cashew tree hadn't shrunk into a month old tree; rather it had become a stump. The mysterious tree had been cut down! Okiki collapsed to his knees, and crawled aimlessly around the tree. He did not want to believe his eyes. He searched everywhere. The cashew tree branches had been cut into pieces and taken away, the fruits were no more there too. Okiki could properly see the handwork of some farmers on the spot. It was real. The cashew tree was gone.

Okiki began to wail. He called out to the cashew tree several times, and got no response. The rough edges of the stump made him sick to the stomach. The horrendous act made his eyes twirl all over. He felt the clouds were scurrying across the sky. And the heavens were turning dark. He seemed to be swept all over by a cold breeze. He shuddered. Suddenly he heard some footsteps coming. Okiki sprang to his feet, dusted himself down, and went home.

Amope noticed something was wrong with Okiki when he arrived. She saw the dry patches of tears across his face. And she wondered what went wrong at school. Okiki refused to say anything, after his mother enquired about his change of disposition towards everyone in the house. Amope decided to give the matter a rest, she felt since he told her about his favourite class-teacher that left several weeks back, probably he was still thinking about her.

That night, Okiki wished it was just a nightmare. He wished it was just a bad dream; a cheap threat that held no water. The following morning, on his way to school, he realised that the cashew tree had actually been cut down. He remained calm, as he did not want his younger friends to suspect a thing. Days after, the village children began spreading the news on why the cashew tree was cut down, but Okiki did not care to listen. The village children all missed the cashew fruits, not the tree.

Days followed, and Okiki began to lose concentration in class. He lost passion for everything and he kept more to himself. Debisi could not draw him out of his shell. And he insisted on saying nothing to his mother. His mind was filled with empty thoughts about the cashew tree, and he could not assimilate. The worries began to tell on his appetite and his health too. Okiki finally broke down with fever.

Amope was thrown into a state of confusion. Her last child hardly fell sick. But this one was worse. Okiki battled with fever for four weeks. Debisi ran around to get all the necessary herbs meant for curing fever. Okiki scooped down herbal concoctions. And he also mixed some with his bathing water every day. As the weeks went by, the young boy regained his strength and his consciousness too.

Okiki remembered all the advice he had received from the cashew tree. And he carefully fit them together in his life's puzzle. The cashew tree had once explained to him that the path to greatness was lonely and filled with obstacles. Okiki could clearly remember when the mysterious tree told him that obstacles were not events that stop people from achieving their goals in life, rather they were events that kept people's eyes off their goals. Sudden mishaps were bound to happen. But the ultimate joy is when people achieved their dreams. Okiki now understood better, and he felt so sorry for putting his mother and sister through so much trouble. Okiki's health returned, and he went back to pursue his dreams.

Okiki's outstanding brilliance was clearly admired by his new class-teacher too. The man helped him in every way he needed, and was sure Okiki would excel in his final exams. Okiki and the rest of the final year students sat for the Secondary School Entrance Examination and the Scholarship exam too, at the end of the session. They all went home, and awaited their results.

At first, Okiki felt jittery, as he awaited his results, but the excitement around him quickly choked up such feelings. His fame had spread across the village, and more village children started coming to Amope's hut to be groomed by Okiki for admission into the Missionary school in the coming session.

"Someday, our village would also have a primary school." Amope teased.

"The first set of children that joined school was five, now it's almost twelve that would be joining too." Okiki added.

"Probably Okiki would become the first village school teacher," Debisi teased.

And they all laughed loudly. Okiki couldn't have wished for anything better. He had set a legacy across the village, and others were now treading the path. Truly, someday, Irewolu village would have its own schools, and someday too, it would develop into an urban environment, and probably a city. Okiki wished he would be available to do more for his place of birth, but that dream may not come true presently, because Doja would be coming back in a few weeks to take him to the city for his secondary education.

It was the day Doja arrived back from the city that Okiki's results came out. The return of Doja had caused so much bubbling in the family. They would be travelling to the city the next day. But the expectation towards Okiki's result that day had caused so much excitement. Amope promised to cook a special dish for Okiki on his return back from school.

A lot of price had been paid. Okiki remembered it all, as he returned back to the village later in the afternoon. Setting forth at dawn to the next village five times a week; covering kilometres by foot. The once little boy who had now metamorphosed into a young boy, remembered it all as he held his excellent results in his hand. Not only did he excel, he also qualified for the scholarship. He was in high spirits as he held his admission letter.

"Thank you." Okiki said, as he reached the spot where the cashew tree once stood proudly.

He stopped for a while. He looked at the stump and saw that a node was already swelling out from the stump of the cashew tree. Okiki was delighted; the cashew tree was coming back to life. He called out and hoped to hear a response; even if it was a faint one. But he heard nothing. The measure of support he got from the mysterious tree could not be overestimated. Okiki wished they could rejoice together at that moment. He had all the time in the world. And so he waited a little longer; probably the cashew tree might give him some parting words too. But he still did not hear a thing. And so, he ran home joyfully.

The speed and air that Okiki carried back to his hut that afternoon suddenly vanished. Okiki halted, as he saw a few people scattered across their compound. No one took notice of him, as their heads hung low and their countenance was melancholic. The last time he saw such a sight was the day his father was brought home dead. His heart beat increased, as he walked slowly towards the hut.

As he got closer, he caught sight of his sister, Debisi being held by two strong women as she wailed. The two women tried to comfort Debisi, and the words Okiki heard showed that a sudden disaster had actually occurred in their home. He doubled his pace, and walked past the people outside. Before they caught wind of Okiki or hold him back, he was already in the hut.

"Wait, Okiki!" Doja called out, as he turned around.

But Okiki was too fast for them all. The young boy screamed and ran out of the hut. Okiki screamed when he caught sight of his mother lying peacefully still across the floor. Her face was calm and shut. But Okiki could also see fresh bruises across her body. His mother had suffered another epilepsy fit, he could tell. Two elderly men stood around Amope, and Doja knelt before her body. Okiki had to strain above Doja's shoulders to see the dried patches of blood flitted around Amope's mouth and neck. The young boy had first restrained his feelings, but when Doja covered

Amope's face with a piece of white cloth, Okiki knew the chain had snapped, and the golden lamp had fallen and broken. Amope was dead.

Okiki kept running. He cried loudly as he ran. Tears stained his face, and blurred his sight. He dashed his foot across creeping weeds and pelted stones away as he ran, but he did not fall. The cashew tree could see Okiki coming. The mysterious tree was regaining its strength, and could see what Okiki was about to do. The wise tree called out the young boy's name, but he did not hear. Okiki ran past the stump of the cashew tree, and kept running. Okiki ran out of the village, out of the market square, onto the next village. He swiped at the blades of grasses and creeping weeds, as he ran up the hill. He halted when he got to the top of the hill.

He fell under the acacia tree and wailed loudly. The place was quiet and deserted, and no one could locate him there. He screamed and cursed, as past memories flashed across his face. His mother had risked her marriage, her life, and her well-being towards his success. She believed in him so much, and he also believed someday he would wipe away her tears. Okiki also realised if Amope had agreed to follow Doja back to the city when the latter suggested, probably she would not have died. But she had decided to stay with him, until the end of his school year.

"Mother, why?" Okiki yelled.

His voice echoed across the hill. And he could also hear his own voice far below; on the surface of the stream. Suddenly, Okiki sprang to his feet. He hurried to the edge of the hill, and could see the quiet stream flowing gently far below. Okiki attempted to dive into the stream, but he missed his steps, and slipped. The young boy fell with his face downwards and saw as pebbles toppled over the hill into the stream.

A tinge of cowardice swept over him. He could hear his heart beating faster. Okiki yelled, and burst into another round of laughter. He wondered why he was unable to hurt his life. He took a glance at the stream far below and saw many ripples across its surface. Okiki sniggered as the ripples struck a chord in his mind. He had seen ripples several times, but the first day Mary brought him up the hill, and the discussion they had over the ripples had remained glued to his mind. The young boy wiped his crumpled eyes, and sat down to think.

Okiki remembered how Mary had described the ripples as the adversities of life which would only last for a short while. He equally remembered his favourite teacher had also likened it to the impact people make during their lifetime. He also remembered the mysterious tree had warned him that life was a gift that must not be wasted. Okiki leaned backwards, and stared at the skies. The young boy came to terms with the fact that he might not be able to control what happened around him, but he could certainly control what happened to him.

Amope's death had cut a gash in his heart. But committing suicide wasn't a solution either. Okiki understood his mother's abrupt death would remain indelible in his heart. But taking his own life would have destroyed the dreams of so many village children who believed in him, while his own existence was a leverage upon which others could build their dreams. Okiki sighed loudly and cleared his mind. For the first time he was making a lifetime decision all by himself. Even though life had dealt him the wrong cards, but fulfilling his dreams, and becoming a great role model shined brightly on his mind.

The sun began to sink slowly, and the clouds began to crawl away from the sky. Okiki had spent a long time on the hill, and the evening was drawing nearer. He realised how worried his elder brother and sister must have been by then. He sprang up and hurried down the hill. The journey back home was quite long and dreary, but Okiki was ready to make it.

ACKNOWLEDGMENTS

THANKS TO THE Creator, for the gift of life, and also for turning this dream into reality. Thanks to my publishing team and my young cousin; Tosin Alabi–for working with me from the first draft to this final one. All persisting errors and imperfections in this novel are mine.

Special thanks, to my parents; Jola and Yinka Oyeku for providing me with an educated background and a stimulating environment that spurred my creativity. And a personal prostration to my dad for favours immeasurable. A big hug to Oladele Oyeku, for blood and love; more hugs to Bukola Alabi, for a heartfelt friendship and respect.

Thanks to Wole Soyinka, Chinua Achebe, Ngugi wa Thiong'o, and every African writer, whose works have nurtured my soul and paved a way for the future writers. Thanks to Omotayo Fadina, Ayoola Oyeniyi, Wole Awoleke and Demola Babatunde, for a memorable friendship and a writing bond. *In loving memory* of Kayode Moliki and Tolu Oduwole (2001), the fond memories remain evergreen on my mind.

To Joke Alabi, June Obiago, and Dele Akinbode, for benevolence and invaluable support; To Kunle Adesanwo, Ayomide Sokunbi, Abdulsalami Ladigbolu, Seun Ajayi, Olaolu Okunola, Ayobami Iyiola and Bolaji Ajani, for friendship and faith. Am thankful to everyone I have had contact with, especially my friends on the social networking sites. God bless you.

A NOTE ABOUT THE AUTHOR

AYO OYEKU IS a Nigerian writer. He showed his early niche for writing in 2004 when he published two children storybooks; *First Among Equals* and *Noble Ambition*. Afterwards, his writings started appearing in various anthologies across the globe. His commitment to nation building, earned him the State Leadership for the Read and Earn Campaign Team (REC). He is a member of the International Who's Who of Professionals, International Young Professionals Foundation (IYPF), Association of Nigerian Authors (ANA) and other notable organisations. He divides his time between writing, nation building and entrepreneurship. This is his first novel.

Readers are encouraged to visit the novel website www. tearsofthelonely.com for comments and updates. Thanks.